Naming The Frame

Naming
The
Frame

Why Christians need
the bigger picture

Jonathan Ingleby

Wide Margin

The definition of alienation is something along the lines that people have no overview over the context in which they live their lives, no perspective on the threads that hold their lives together.
(Andri Snær Magnason in *Dreamland*)

The critical hermeneutical principle is the context

To my daughter, Kate, who has consistently
chosen challenging contexts for her life
and lived accordingly

CONTENTS

INTRODUCTION

I had a Maths teacher many years ago who used to put a complicated geometric proof on the blackboard and then comment: 'That seems quite straightforward to me.' Well, it may have seemed straightforward to him, but it did not make much sense to me!

In the end, most of us would agree that life is not all that easy to understand, that the messages we receive from within and from others and from God are not always clear. As the Apostle Paul famously said; 'Now we see in a mirror dimly (one translation has 'in a riddle')', always remembering that mirrors in the ancient world gave a very distorted image. It is partly that all our messages are filtered through to us by our language and culture, but even more because we are fallible and sinful creatures.

This last compounds the situation. Our proneness to error means that our cultures are also fallen. We cannot appeal to them as some sort of infallible divine appointment. In truth we are fallible human beings living in equally 'broken' cultures and yet depending on those cultures for the 'translation' of the messages about life that we receive. No wonder we are in a mess.

If this is true there are at least two important consequences. Those who claim they have absolute certainty should be treated with caution. It is right that we should be suspicious. When it comes to divine messages, for example, the Apostle Paul has a distinctly 'suspicious' approach. 'Let two or three prophets speak, and let the others weigh what is said', he says to the church in Corinth (1 Corinthians 14:29) or again, writing to the Thessalonians, he encourages them to listen to 'prophetic utterances' but he also asks them to 'test everything' (1 Thessalonians 5:20,21).

The second consequence, and the more important one for this book, is that it follows that the more we study and understand the context, the better we shall understand the message. If messages are mediated to us through our cultures, a process that colours and even distorts the message, we need to examine the culture in order, so to speak, to undo the damage, and 'straighten out' the communication.

Here is a very simple example. Leaders of a particular church decided to remove the original pews in their church building and to replace them by more flexible seating arrangements. This action was met by an almost uncontrolled fury from a widow in the congregation, a woman not at all known for outbursts of this sort. What had been done, she said, was wrong, and there was nothing more to say about it. But of course there was. What the church leaders needed to understand was the *context* if they were to *interpret* the situation. The woman's late husband had always sat with her in a particular pew during church services. To remove the pew was to remove one of the solid shared memories that she had of their life together. If the leaders had understood the context they would have understood the woman's behaviour.

So what I want to do in this book is to look at a number of ways in which context needs to be taken as fully into account as we can. This will not solve every riddle, of course. Knowing why the woman was angry did not tell the church leaders exactly what to do about it. Understanding context is like learning a foreign language. Without the language in a foreign country we are reduced to the state of know-nothings. Even children have the advantage over us. While knowing the language will not automatically mean that we conduct our business successfully or have a good holiday, one can easily see that it might help.

There is something much deeper here. The greatest example of paying attention to the context is the Incarnation, when the Word became flesh in a particular place at a particular time, a theme I shall develop as we go along. But an incarnational ministry is a costly thing and we have all sorts of ways of avoiding it. So often we have retreated into a Christian 'island culture' which does not connect with 'the mainland'. Sadly, some groups have made a deliberate choice to be 'separate' and put structures in place to make sure this stance is retained, but all Christian groups are at risk of becoming isolated. The company of other Christians is, not surprisingly, often more congenial than that of non-Christians, and the temptation is to spend all our 'out-of-office' hours with them. Church activities can become absorbing. A final step may be going into 'full-time Christian service' where we minister in a church or run a Christian agency and never have much to do with non-Christians at all.

Sometimes we have moved so decisively into the Christian culture that we no longer understand what 'ordinary' people live by—what are their hopes and fears, their joys and their sorrows. Indeed we do not really understand their language, even though we can all speak English!

If we know little about our neighbours we often know even less about the big issues of the day. We live in a complex and confusing world, but have we made much effort to acquire the tools to make an adequate exploration of it? And I do not necessarily mean theological tools (though that would be a good starting place) but some sort of basic grasp of economics or sociology or politics. Indeed we do not even read the newspaper or watch the news on TV.

In brief, we seem unable to connect, and to be fair, it is not just Christians. There is a widespread feeling among folk that the world at large, outside of our own families, jobs and social life, is not really one that we can influence in a meaningful way. Zygmunt Bauman in his helpful book *The Individualized Society* uses an apt illustration. What was once true was that we all thought of ourselves as potential pilgrims. Whatever the obstacles, the task was to proceed with determination along the track stretching ahead. There might be trials, disappointments, even failures, but the goal was clear. (Think of Pilgrim in *Pilgrim's Progress* or Frodo in *Lord of the Rings*.)

But the problem today is that we feel much more like drop-outs, or people with no fixed purpose in life. The daily question is not 'How can I get to my next destination?' but 'Where could I, or should I, go? And where will this road I've taken bring me?' The task is to pick the least risky turn at the nearest crossroads or to change direction before the road ahead gets impassable. (Bauman 2001, 147) This bears directly on the way that we plan the future. We have been dis-empowered. What is the point of planning at all, if we do not see that the future can be made significantly different by anything that we can do? There is real power about and we feel its effects, but it is global, extraterritorial power, so to speak, that we cannot access. We remain 'attached to the ground' (Bauman 2001, 149). Action is not just incurably localised, it is also privatised and individualised. Because we believe that we cannot do what really matters, we turn to things that matter less, but which we can control. As Christopher Lasch has said:

> Having no hope of improving their lives in any of the ways that matter, people have convinced themselves that what matters is psychic self-improvement; getting in touch with their feelings, eating health food, taking lessons in ballet or belly-dancing, immersing themselves in the wisdom of the East, jogging, learning how to 'relate', overcoming the 'fear of pleasure'. Harmless in themselves, these pursuits, elevated to a programme and wrapped in the rhetoric of authenticity and awareness, signify a retreat from politics...
> (Bauman 2001, 150)

And we might add, a retreat from building the kingdom of God.

The retreat from politics is not just because we feel helpless; we also feel distrustful. In his book about a possible way forward to a sustainable life-style, Tim O'Riordan writes in the opening chapter (along with

Chris Church) about the growing feeling that we have that we cannot *trust* our leaders. He cites the research done by a team at Princeton University (Puttnam et al. 2000) which analyses current democracies and attempts to assess the public response to issues of trust and representation. The conclusion is, put simply, that the level of trust is falling dramatically, and that this is almost universal. This applies to the USA and Great Britain and to continental Europe, including such apparently successful democracies as Sweden, where, according to the researchers, a 51 per cent confidence in the Swedish parliament was lowered to a mere 19 per cent during the decade of 1985-1995 (O'Riordan 2001, 10).

The truth is, of course, that our leaders are probably no more or less trustworthy than they have ever been. It is how we feel about them that has changed. I suspect the same is true of our church leaders, though I have no statistics to prove this. Whatever the reason for this change, it is no secret that lack of trust is a great de-motivator. Why should we bother, people say, when even our leaders are not trustworthy people?

In the light of this disempowerment, the question is where do we start. As far as the teaching of the church is concerned, I suggest that the task is to remind people, as vividly as we can, that the time has come for *us* to take the responsibility. We cannot afford to be cynical about the society in which we live or indifferent to the fate of the planet. Nor is it sufficient to have vague aspirations. We need to be clear about the mission of the church and the part we can play in it. Admittedly, in the twenty-first century, it is not all that easy to know what we mean by this. The word 'mission' does not stand for something quite obvious and explicable. When people say that they have 'a heart for mission' I am always inclined to think—'good, but what comes next?' After all the word 'mission' simply implies that someone is about to be sent somewhere. But where are we being sent and to what purpose?

The Apostle Paul had a strongly developed sense of purpose! He talked about 'fighting the fight' and 'finishing the race'. He thought there was a prize waiting for him (2 Timothy 4:7-8). He wanted to 'achieve' the resurrection (Philippians 3:11). He spoke, in Ephesians 6, about a struggle which is not against human enemies but against spiritual forces. He realised that he was up against 'powers' that were much stronger than he was. So this *defined* the struggle. My hope is that studying our context may help us to identify the powers that are threatening us, and that thereby we may define our struggle.

What 'race' did Paul have in mind? In his address to the elders of the church at Ephesus he said that for him 'finishing the course' had to do with passing on 'the whole purpose of God' (Acts 20:24, 27). He had a message and his goal was to make sure that the next generation knew what that message was. In doing this he was fulfilling his part of the Great Commission. When we listen to Jesus defining mission for his followers in Matthew 28 we find that he sends them into all the world 'to make disciples'. Now the world is full of 'disciples', but the eleven men there on the mountain had a quite specific teaching job. They were to teach 'all the things that Jesus had commanded'.

Just think about that for a moment! Think about the Sermon on the Mount and the parables of the kingdom and the teaching about 'the coming of the Son of Man' and the need to be ready—it was their (and our) mission to pass on all that. So, as we have said, 'mission' needs defining. You are sent somewhere, to someone, with a certain message and to do certain things. In another sense, it is following Jesus, and that is what 'sets the agenda' best of all. In yet another sense it is 'passing on the message'.

Mission also has a context. Go into 'all the world' says Jesus. Understanding our world helps us to see more clearly where the path of discipleship might lie and what that message we are to pass on might be. Paul had a vision of a man from Macedonia who said 'come over and help us' (Acts 16:9). He had, at least for the time being, a Macedonian context. What did God want Paul to help the Macedonians with? Well there was a fortune telling girl, kept as a slave like a pet monkey, and she needed delivering from her masters (Acts 16:16f.). (And how many people are kept in slavery today by ruthless and money grabbing owners and need some help to get free?) There was also a group of Jewish women who met 'outside the city gate' (you had to have *men* if you are going to form a synagogue) and they needed to be incorporated more fully into the people of God (Acts 16:13-15). Again, there was a town gaoler who needed to be 'saved' but did not really know what that meant, but probably guessed that the men he was dealing with had been unjustly imprisoned (Acts 16:30). Immediately Paul answers the call mission begins, and immediately he is in the battle, a battle which involves exploitive labour, discrimination against women, and unjust practices.

Look about you. What do you see? Your circumstances may not seem very exciting, certainly when compared to what happened to Paul at Philippi. Yet something very dramatic is going on all the same. Arundhati Roy puts it this way:

> It's not war, it's not genocide, it's not ethnic cleansing, it's not famine or an epidemic. On the face of it, it's just ordinary day-to-day business. It lacks the drama, the large-format, epic magnificence of war or genocide. It's dull by comparison. It makes bad T.V. It has to do with boring things like water supply, electricity, irrigation. But it also has to do with the process of barbaric dispossession on a scale that has few parallels in history. You may have guessed by now that I'm talking about the modern version of globalisation.
> (Roy 2002, 177)

In John 20:21 Jesus said to his disciples 'As the Father sent me, so I am sending you.' (That 'sending' word again!) So, once again, our mission is like his. The passage also tells us that 'he showed them his hands and his side'. The mission of Jesus had to do with suffering. But then so does ours. What Arundhati Roy calls 'globalisation' speaks not simply of some economic and political system but of a world in turmoil, a world where there are 100 million street children, where a billion people every morning wake up hungry, where we are daily beating our ploughshares into swords and our pruning hooks into spears in the name of the false god 'security'. It is into *this* world that we are sent.

I hope that I have already at this stage successfully introduced to you some of the themes of this book, namely the dangers of withdrawal and the need to attend faithfully to the context. 'Living in context', as it might be described, is worth doing if it reminds us that we are in a battle, indeed in a struggle for survival. It is worth doing if it tunes us into the world's suffering and our part in it as followers of the 'suffering servant'. It is worth doing if it gives us a new sense of urgency. 'The end of all things is near' as the Apostle Peter says, 'be serious and discipline yourselves' (1 Peter 4:7). Above all, it will have served its purpose if it challenges us to be better disciples of Jesus 'in this present age'.

LIVING IN CONTEXT:
SOME DEFINITIONS

Living

This chapter began life as an article called 'I Came, I Saw...I Had No Idea What To Do Next'. No doubt we would all like to be 'living in context' but the truth is that, for many of us, defining *how* we should live is precisely the problem. We can see that something needs to be done, and do not want to be accused of hardheartedness or indifference, but the pathway we need to take seems unclear. Recently I went to an excellent presentation of anti-war poetry. It took the line, precisely opposed to Auden's famous assertion that 'poetry makes nothing happen'[1], that 'rhyme is still the most effective drum'. As I listened to the verse I felt angry and sad, at times appalled. But I didn't really know what to *do*.

About the same time I heard a sermon which powerfully reminded us that many of the world's woes—particularly to do with the gap between the rich and the poor—are *our* responsibility. It is we in the West who are living extravagantly at the expense of our poorer neighbours. We cannot 'pass by on the other side' like the priest and the Levite in the parable. But, again, what was it that we were being challenged to do?

1 From W. H. Auden's poem 'In Memory of W. B. Yeats'.

The sermon was actually mainly about our responsibilities in view of the environmental crisis. So here was a third issue. We are all scrambling to do the right thing, to reduce our 'carbon footprint', to recycle and not live wastefully. And yet we feel rather helpless. It is like being on a runaway train. The key issue is not what the passengers do, but who has access to the controls and whether they can apply the brakes. (Ingleby 2010b, 10)

I have already mentioned three 'big issues': war and violence, the gap between rich and poor and the environmental crisis. There are many more issues of this sort, of course, but I want to use these as 'typical' debating points. About each of these issues I suggest that there are at least five questions to be asked and answered. (1) What are the facts? (2) What do they mean? (3) What ought we to do? (4) Can we do it? (5) Will it make any difference?

Let me begin on a sceptical note and try to reproduce some of the arguments I have heard which suggest that there is *nothing* we can do. Here are some of the voices.

- Being against war in a general sense is one thing, but does that require us to be out-and-out pacifists? There are evil people about, and sometimes armed forces are necessary to protect us from them. Think for example of the Second World War when we were fighting against Hitler. Evil is a fact of life; it is not what we would wish, but we have no choice but to respond to it. There are good wars and bad wars. People like us are usually not in a position to decide between them, and so, quite reasonably, we leave the decisions to the people we have elected who know more about these things than we do.

• The business about the rich and the poor is also tricky. Take the matter of overseas aid. We are always being exhorted to contribute to good causes but there is apparently a great deal of evidence that (a) the aid does not get through to the people for whom it is intended (b) even when it does, it can easily do more harm than good, creating unreal expectations and real dependencies. Also, we have noticed that there is a growing volume of disapproving comment aimed at the aid agencies both government and non-government. Governments are often corrupt, and non-government organisations (NGOs) attract a number of criticisms: they create artificial markets (for example, food aid encourages local people not to produce food); they employ a local relatively well-paid elite who are alienated from their own people; they drain off crucial resources and personnel from government agencies, and so on. On a really big scale, the major players such as the World Bank are widely believed to be the agents of Western monetary and trade policy, wielding their huge influence on behalf of the already too rich and powerful G8 countries.

• Besides, I am not a social scientist. I have never studied Development Economics. Who do I believe, anyway? I read neither the *Economist*[2] nor the *New Internationalist*[3], but if I did, I suspect

2 A weekly magazine largely representing the point of view of the business world.

3 A monthly magazine taking a radical or left-wing stance and specialising in issues to do with the Global South.

I would get almost diametrically opposed viewpoints on these issues. And suppose I was clear in my thinking and had decided that the time had come for me to contribute to Oxfam or write to my MP, would it really make much difference in the great scheme of things?

• I find it even more depressing that at times there *is* no obvious right and wrong. Suppose *all* the supermarkets are keeping prices down by paying unfair prices to producers and exploiting cheap labour. Suppose *all* the oil companies are operating as gangsters. What if Big Pharma is a world-wide racket, making huge profits on the back of people's ignorance, fear and need? Where then do I go to buy food for my table, or petrol for my car, or drugs when I am ill?

• It also seems reasonable that we have to attend to our own needs first. There are plenty of people in our 'home' countries below the poverty line, plenty of disturbed families, people on drugs, disabled people, dropouts, old folks with nobody to look after them, unemployed, single mothers. Some of them live right next door to me. What about higher food and fuel prices, floods, domestic violence, uncontrolled immigration, discrimination against women, increasing pollution, paedophilia, gun and knife crime? This is no time to be thinking about Afghanistan (except when one of our soldiers has been lost), or Congo, or Myanmar.

• The environmental crisis is palpably one for the politicians to solve. However much I insulate the loft, drive a smaller car, buy locally produced food, it will make very little difference if the US,

China, India, Europe and the rest do not find a way of reducing our dependence on fossil fuels, to mention just one significant environmental issue. The scale of the problem is global not personal.

• So let's forget about the big issues like war and inequality and the environment. We are not sure what the truth is half the time. Even when that is sorted out, there is so much need that it is impossible to work out the priorities. Surely, for most of us, the big issues will have to give way to the smaller ones, issues that affect us directly and which we can handle. Charity begins at home, does it not? Obviously war, and inequality and the environment are important, but I am a 'little person' and these are big issues that will have to be left to the 'big people'.

I hear these voices—indeed some of them are my own—and yet I also believe that we can answer our five questions more positively.

It is just possible that our first task (establishing the facts) is the most important area of all. This should come as an encouragement to those of us who seldom get any further. When people understand that they are being deceived, or that they are prospering at the expense of others, or that it is their children and grandchildren who will reap the consequences of this generation's foolish actions, then they will begin to act more wisely and to support those who act wisely on their behalf. If this is true then the most important roles belong to prophets, teachers, preachers, authors, poets, artists and the like. When we think of the ministry of Jesus we need to remember that he was primarily a teacher who had a group of disciples. Also that he spent a good deal of time just warning people. Al Gore missed out on being President of the United States but perhaps producing the documentary 'An Inconvenient Truth'[4] and propagating it world-wide was actually a more significant role. It is not wrong that we should be dissatisfied with theory that never results in action, but it is wrong that we should minimise the theoretician's role. Sometimes, the answer to the question 'What shall we do?' is quite simply 'spread the word'.

Ignorance is the excuse we make, but it is not a very good one. Studying is open to all of us. We can find out a great deal about most things simply by taking a good hard look. Tough, complex issues are not necessarily impossibly mysterious; they just need more work. Often more knowledge is available than we admit. Our ignorance is culpable. I recently read an extended essay on the life of Wilhelm Klemperer, a Jewish intellectual whose diary gives us a vivid picture of life under the Third Reich in Germany. It was commonly believed after the 1939-45 War that during the Reich many Germans simply did not know how the Jews were being treated by the Nazis. Apparently this was not the case. 'Ordinary' people were well aware of the facts. Klemperer himself, restricted in his access to information in many ways, knew about the concentration camps and what was going on there. However hard the 'powers' tried to conceal unwelcome truths, they got out. I think this applies today in many situations. Cover-ups seldom work with complete efficiency.

4 A film warning about the dangers of global warming,

Keeping abreast and being informed is good work, but it is also hard work. In an effort to do so I take a daily newspaper and four journals. An evening with any one of them usually makes me feel fatigued and depressed. It is not so much that most of the news is bad—though that is certainly the case—it is more that people can write with considerable insight and knowledge about all sorts of world events, and yet there seems no acknowledgement of anything remotely transcendent at all. Everything is explicable within a narrow range of human motivation. There are value judgements, of course, indeed most of the writers have a strong sense of good and evil, but their means of discrimination are painfully self-referential—'we hold these truths to be self evident' because they are *our* truths, and that seems to be the limit of it. Nothing is, or can be, said about God, or judgement, or absolutes, or for that matter about miracle, or grace, or mercy. Everything has a meaning, but it is a meaning within a narrow world-view, a sort of discourse, which seizes power in 'the war of myths' (in which, God knows, we are all involved) by wielding knowledge like an axe that cuts down anything that looks like a sacred grove. To use another metaphor: reading in this mode is like being gradually asphyxiated, as the air I habitually breathe is replaced by another foreign element, which my Christian lungs cannot draw upon. No wonder I come away fatigued and depressed.

You might say at this stage—and with some justice—that there is a simple remedy. Stop reading the stuff. Read some book or journal where the air has more oxygen, where God, judgement, absolutes,

miracle, grace, mercy and the like are freely acknowl-
edged and talked about. I do read such authors, and
probably would not survive without them, but this
solution to my dilemma is only a partial one. The difficulty is that I am not so much seeking withdrawal as
connection.

For the last twenty years or so I have been a full-
time, professional missiologist. Missiology can be
briefly described as the study of how God is at work in
the world and how we can join Him in that work. Now
you will readily see that the last thing that this allows
me to do is withdraw. In prosaic terms, I need to know
what is going on. I need to read the newspaper and
watch the television. Better still, I need to be involved
myself, but that is another story. I suppose it would
be fine if we had a range of Christian authors who
were giving us quality analysis of the news and who
had the ability (and courage) to express this from
within the 'prophetic' worldview—a latter day Amos
or Isaiah in fact. I think there are such, but they are
not many, and, to my knowledge, they do not provide
a sustained commentary on current events.

This is the dilemma. There is plenty of informed
analysis, much of it impressive in its detail, written
from within the 'secular' discourse. The journals and
books that I regularly read on current events do in
fact have much that I want and need to know, and
could not find elsewhere.

Why is there such a disparity between the two
sources of information? Obviously, to some extent, it
reflects that, in the West at least, the Christian presence has now dwindled to quite a small minority. We

simply do not have the resources to provide the sort of coverage that our majority (secular) culture can offer. But there is something else. For far too long the church has simply shied away from the task, often finding spurious theological justifications for this behaviour. We think that we can live within the 'private' and that the 'public' is not really our business, forgetting perhaps that our private world has become powerless *because* we Christians have abandoned public discourse.

It will be evident from what I have just written that in this search for 'the facts' we constantly come up against the question: 'are we able to interpret them correctly?' The question of 'spin' or 'bias' is a crucial one when we are trying to work out the rights and wrongs of a situation. Remember the run-up to the Iraq war? Simply stated, we needed to decide whether this was a good war or a bad one. The alarming thing was that we never really found out what the issues were until after the troops had gone in. Apparently we were deceived, but knowing that now simply indicates that we did not have the information we needed at the time. In fact that information was being withheld from us. The role of those who inform us is important because there are false messages as well as truthful ones. We are so often at the mercy of the 'spin-doctors'—politicians, newspaper owners and their employees, radio and TV pundits, and more generally what we call the 'media', including advertising, popular fiction, TV drama and films. It is a struggle to know where the truth lies. But that is the point—it is a struggle. It is something we have to work at.

In the Joseph story in the Old Testament when he is in prison with the officials, the ability to interpret is evidently the key to the action. The facts are known—both officials remember their dreams clearly enough—but the big question is: 'What do they mean?' As Joseph said 'Do not interpretations belong to God?' (Genesis 40:8). Perhaps we Christians actually have an advantage here. The Apostle Paul, in Acts 16, did not know what was next on the agenda, until he had a vision of a man from Macedonia saying 'come over and help us'. I am not saying that we should wait for a vision before we get down to work. I am saying that 'interpretations belong to God'. When we are confused about the meaning of something and what we should do about it, we can at least ask!

The third question 'what *ought* we to do?' in the sense of what is our moral responsibility as Christian disciples, is a very challenging one. The hard thing to say—hard, but true—is that we often stop at this point because of the cost. We say we are confused or disillusioned, that we are not sure that what has been proposed is going to work, but the real reason for our inaction is our unwillingness to pay the price in terms of our standard of living, our use of time, our personal preferences and our convenience. Consider:

 • I don't think I should be shopping at supermarkets but shopping elsewhere is more expensive and supermarket shopping fits more conveniently into my scheduling—so don't ask me to change.

 • I really think fair trade is a good idea but I can't afford fair trade prices.

- I am not entirely happy about working in the weapons' industry, but it's difficult to find good jobs around here.

- I realise that my carbon footprint is rather heavy and that frequent flights contribute to that, but I deserve a good holiday and you can't trust the weather in this country.

Now, I am not saying that supermarkets are wrong, or that we always have to buy fair trade products, or that it is unethical to work for the arms industry or that taking regular holiday flights is a moral outrage. I am not judging these issues one way or another. I leave that to people's consciences. What I am saying is that if you do think that they are wrong then the reasons given here for doing them are inadequate. As we all know, principles are costly, and if they cost us nothing then they are probably not our principles. The Apostle Paul said on one occasion—just as he was about to begin a defence of his whole life and ministry before a highly critical audience—'I thank God whom I serve with a good conscience' (Acts 23:1). Paul did not mean by this that he always got things right. He meant rather that he was a man of integrity. He was serving God in such a way that no one could accuse him of believing one thing and doing another or of acting from base motives. This is not too high a standard for us to aim at. In such complex matters as war, social inequality and the environment we shall by no means always make the right decisions. But woe betide us if we believe something to be right and yet find selfish or fearful reasons for not doing it. We need a 'good conscience' before we attempt to tackle the big issues.

Can we do what needs to be done when faced by complex moral issues, or to put it another way, is what we propose to do likely to make any difference? Undoubtedly the answer is sometimes 'no'. We may have established the facts, interpreted them correctly, found the will to act upon them, set aside feeble excuses, and we may still find that we are not free to move forward. We live in a world in which the (evil) structures we inhabit are often stronger than we are. I suspect that many Germans wanted to save their Jewish neighbours in the 1930s but were simply unable to do so. A million people protested against the second Iraq war, but it did not stop the bombers going in.

Evil practices may be beyond our geographical reach or our intellectual grasp or they may be intertwined with other factors from which they cannot be disentangled. I often tell the story of the child labourers who lived and worked near us in India, and were employed in the match and firework industry at great cost to their health. We thought about mounting some sort of campaign against this until we realised that the local agriculture had failed so disastrously that to remove even this meagre income from the families —the income from their children's employment, that is—would be to condemn the families to starvation. What needed to be done about the failed agriculture, we had no idea.

And yet... and yet...

First of all, it is important not to be overwhelmed by the issues. If we start with the little issues we may find that they lead in due course to the big ones, indeed that they are the same ones and cannot be dealt with separately. Because I cannot do everything it does not mean that I cannot do anything. Because I am not God it does not mean that I can abdicate my humanity. Equally, doing something does not mean that I have to do everything. It is reasonable to select some issues and ignore others. This is akin to God's question to Moses: 'What is in your hand?' (Exodus 4:2). Where precisely do we already have influence? Perhaps our church could 'go green' or our workplace could become a fair-trade zone. We all have our special interests, our areas of expertise and our distinct callings and giftings. Ignoring immediate and pressing cries for help (think of the parable of the Good Samaritan) may be wrong, but we should not feel guilty about getting involved with issues that are congenial to us, or where we know that we can be particularly effective.

Some of the resources that are currently available favour 'little people agendas'. The Internet, for example, allows people who may be very much in the minority in their own communities to link up with likeminded people world-wide. Cheap travel does the same. The rich and powerful can have their annual conference at Davos[5], but the World Social Forum[6] is also possible. In general what sociologists call 'reflexivity' is on the increase. The little people can insist that they have their say. In the present climate 'Because I told you so' will not work any longer, nor

5 World leaders—politicians, media barons, military top brass, leading economists etc.—meet every year in the Swiss resort of Davos to exchange ideas and discuss policy.
6 An annual gathering of left-wing and radical activists. Based to-date in Brazil it will in future be decentralised.

will 'just do it'. The media are alive to this. We, the public, are constantly being invited to join the discussion via 'phone-ins, e-mail messages, letter pages, and the like, and our votes are expected to override the 'experts'—just think of the way the public is given a vote as part of competitions on the television such as the X Factor. Media celebrities can be brought to heel by the complaints of the public. The ubiquitous public opinion polls suggests that somebody is listening. Perhaps we have assumed too readily that we do not have a voice.

In fact, getting heard may not be as difficult as we think. A book like Mark Thomas's *Belching Out The Devil* (Thomas 2008)– an exposé of Coca Cola—is an example. His research is thorough, but it is not beyond the range of many of us. What makes the difference is his enthusiasm. There are many issues, I suspect, to which we could give a similar public airing, even if it is only a matter of asking some questions. Here are three, selected from the areas of concern that we have pinpointed, which I have wanted to raise recently.

• Is there a legal way of preventing my taxes being spent on Trident? [war]

• How is it that the really cheap shops such as *Matalan* or *Primark*, can sell as cheaply as they do? Is somebody being exploited along the way? [inequality]

• What precisely happens to the waste collected from my doorstep every Monday? [environment]

In each case there is (1) probably something on the internet I could look at; (2) probably somebody among my friends, acquaintances or colleagues that will have some ideas; (3) a possibility of raising the questions directly with the appropriate powers —the local tax authorities, the managers of the relevant shops and the council's waste disposal department. I may be able to see them (best), telephone them (next best) or send them an e-mail or letter (if all else fails). Even if a satisfactory answer is not forthcoming, it is worth establishing how difficult it is to get an answer, a fact in itself worth publicising.

Some while ago I saw a programme on the Television about child labour in the carpet factories of India[7]. At the end it commended the now quite familiar *Rugmark* scheme whereby carpets are given a symbol if the firms that marketed them are able to demonstrate that they are accessing products made in non-exploitive conditions. At the end of the programme it listed a number of participating retailers, including some well known names. So I thought I would do a little experiment. I set out to do the rounds of the local retailers, telling them that I was interested in rugs, but would be pleased to find that they were covered by some sort of fair trade guarantee. None of them were aware of the *Rugmark* scheme, and this included the outlets which had allowed their names to appear on the programme as supporting the scheme. While I suspect I did nothing for the welfare of the children of India, at least it told me something: in the business world, words and deeds are not necessarily the same thing.

---

7 The programme, titled 'Slavery', was produced by Kate Blewitt and Brian Woods and was screened on Channel 4 in 2000.

Supposing, however, we have successfully collected some useful information, then the next question is how to publicise it. Mark Thomas turned his research on Coca Cola into a book. This is probably not what most of us can do, but something at the level of an article in a magazine, a letter to a journal or newspaper, an entry on some website discussion, might be possible. We all have influence of some sort, as I have said. We could prepare a talk for our church fellowship, or simply discuss the issue over coffee with our colleagues at work. If we have done some research, then it would be worth putting it together as a presentation, if only for our own satisfaction. If something has really stirred us, then it is likely that there are other people locally who are 'into' the same issue or issues. Two are better than one, and a crowd is best of all.

This brings me to another point. Christians have a problem, it seems to me, that they want to fight their battles alone, or not at all. The truth is that there are certainly allies out there, but we are choosy about them. This is part of our defensive mentality ('less than conquerors' as someone has put it) which insists that we can only do business with those who agree with us. I am afraid that in many cases this is a cheap trick to make us more comfortable about our inaction. In point of fact, strategic alliances with people who are different from us and yet who want the same good things, can be very heartening and surprisingly effective. Despite our feeling that the whole world is ganging up on us, it is seldom that a situation is all bad, or that all institutions are equally off the rails. Even with those we regard as 'enemies', some behave better than others and we can act accordingly. We may disapprove of supermarkets but if we must shop at them, better the Co-op than Asda (Wal-Mart)[8]. In fact there is nothing wrong with limited goals. We can vote the bad out even if we do not know how to bring in the good.

In working out who we want to work with, we are not likely to get much help from the Church. It is a striking fact that the Church has spent much time in defining its doctrinal position and yet continues to be very uncertain about what the bases of exclusion and inclusion are. Creeds, confessions of faith, catechisms, conciliar statements, statements of belief remain popular and they clearly have a defining purpose (are you for us or against us?) but at the same time they seem blunt tools for the work for which they were apparently designed. Do they really help us to decide who to work with and who to avoid when we are doing God's work?

When we go back to the example and teaching of Jesus we find that this very question is dealt with head on. The disciples saw someone who was casting out demons who was 'not of their number', so they tried to stop him. Jesus rebuked them for this:

> 'Do not stop him, for no one who performs a miracle in my name will be able the next moment to speak evil of me. He who is not against us is on our side.' (Mark 9:39,40 REB)

8 See e.g. 'The Walmartians Have Landed' (Goldsmith 2001, 106-114)

A simple test you might say. If the person is doing something good (casting out a demon, performing a miracle) then, for those of us who also want to do good, he is for us and not against us.

In fact Jesus had already made this point previously in Mark's Gospel. When Jesus' family came to him, probably to try to dissuade him from continuing his ministry, Jesus himself asks the question as to the true nature of the family of God. His own answer is quite simple. True family members are those who do the will of God (Mark 3:35). It is not a matter of standing within a certain tradition or having certain connections or indeed subscribing to certain beliefs, but rather something that is revealed in life style and behaviour. The definition 'anyone who does the will of God' may seem too wide to be useful. However, it does helpfully put the emphasis on the word 'do'. If you see someone doing good things (never mind who they claim to be representing) then get in there and start doing good things with them.

Against this we need, briefly, to put the words of Jesus recorded by Matthew, 'He who is not with me is against me' (Matthew 12:30), particularly as they echo the wording of Mark 9:40, only in reverse. To my mind what Jesus says in Matthew only reinforces the saying in Mark. The key is the context of the two passages. Both are about casting out demons. In the first (Mark), someone is casting out demons and should be allowed to get on with it. The very work that he is doing proclaims that he is 'for Jesus'. In Matthew, however it is Jesus who is casting out demons and he is attacked by the Pharisees, not for what he is doing—all agree that casting out demons is a good thing—but for the power he supposedly invokes (12:24). The Pharisees have put themselves 'against Jesus' precisely because they have failed to see that good works must be the test of fellowship. In other words, if I am doing God's work and others refuse to recognise it, they put themselves 'out of fellowship'. The criterion for fellowship remains the same: 'anyone who does the will of God'.

The big question that this raises is, how do we recognise God's work. In practice I am not sure that this is as difficult as we sometimes pretend that it is. Those who are involved in 'works of mercy' (Matthew 25:31-46) must surely qualify. Food for the hungry, drink for the thirsty, shelter for the homeless, clothing for the destitute, visits for the prisoners: when people are involved in these ministries, Christ is there. We can extend this to all the excellent work in relief and development that goes on in the world today. Those of us who cannot support Oxfam and the like because they are not Christian organisations had better beware. The attempts of church people to define the boundaries of God's work by means of creeds and statements of faith are inappropriate and even wrong. They are done despite the clear teaching of Jesus that we should judge people by their 'fruits'.

All this does not mean that we need to be less sure about what we believe, nor is what I am saying a plea for less theological sophistication. The critical question is, however, what are we using our credal statements for? If we see them as a useful grammar to go with the language of faith and experience, that is one thing. Certainly, one way of better understanding what we believe and declaring or celebrating it, is to reduce it to a series of well considered summary statements. If they are memorably expressed so much the better. However, if they are designed as a weapon to exclude others then our insecurity may betray us. On any mission field we are likely to encounter people who are unable to formulate their Christian faith very clearly or people with whom we disagree. They may not be professing Christians at all. The test remains, however, 'by their fruits you will know them'. This does not mean that we can have 'Christian fellowship' with them. That would be unrealistic. It does not in fact make any statement about the work of salvation in their lives. But their 'good works' are certainly a basis for co-operation.

Inaction is not an acceptable response. All too often people in the West—including Christians, including Evangelicals—live like the people in Sodom, whose sin (according to Ezekiel 16:49) was that she had 'pride, excess of food and prosperous ease, but did not aid the poor and needy'. We simply cannot go on living in our own little insulated world, pretending that we do not know what is going on and that it has nothing to do with us. I particularly target evangelicals partly because they are my own folk, but also because there is a brand of evangelical spirituality which makes it more likely that the big issues of world poverty are overlooked. I say this for a number of reasons.

- Our church life consumes a great deal of our spare time and energy. We are in danger here. The Old Testament prophets spent much of their time castigating those who put religion above righteousness.

• We often feel that the most important work we have to do with our neighbours is evangelism. This may also be another case of our putting religion before righteousness.

• We are not prepared to give up our comfortable lifestyle. Because we have Christian concerns (church, evangelism and so on) we are perhaps able to do this with a better conscience than so-called worldly people.

Taking my Christian faith seriously has too often been transformed into a prolonged exercise in getting myself sorted out, with the emphasis on personal spirituality, self-examination, walking with God, being filled with the Spirit, having my quiet time, worshipping sincerely and freely, forgiving my enemies and the like. In fairness these items are challenging enough. They are not, however, the same thing as helping the poor in their need.

I used to be involved with mission education work and with a number of colleges that specialised in missiology. You would expect people in these colleges, staff and students alike, to be at the forefront of issues such as poverty and justice. This was not necessarily the case. For all the above reasons, and others beside, being involved with preparation for Christian mission does not apparently sensitise people to these particular issues.

How then should we live? I have here some practical suggestions which are designed to meet the need of those of us who are not intending to do anything dramatic!

• Input the right stuff. What magazines do you subscribe to? Do you read a daily newspaper? Are you on the look out for good documentaries on the television? This is not a hugely expensive or arduous process, indeed it can be quite enjoyable.

• Take a stand on a limited number of well thought out issues. You cannot attend to all the world's needs, but that does not mean that nothing is possible.

• Join with other people who feel the way that you do.

• Suggest to your own church that they have a series from the Bible on issues to do with poverty and wealth or social justice.

• Follow up some issue that has really grabbed your imagination by talking to your elected representatives about it. Similarly, take an issue to your local big name retailers. Do it in the name of Christ. Ask to see the manager and begin your conversation by saying, 'As a Christian I am very concerned that (for example) a number of the products on sale in your shop are produced by means of exploitive labour practices.' More positively, if you are concerned about the way small shops are being closed down by their big competitors, switch your church's account (for food, furnishings, D.I.Y. materials, stationery etc.) to local small suppliers and tell the shop owners you are doing it because the church has a concern for local people and their livelihoods. This may genuinely help them to survive as businesses and, I suspect, will be a far more effective witness than dropping a leaflet through the letterbox inviting them to a Christmas service.

• My experience is that one thing leads to another. The more involved I get the more I need to know. (For example, about fair trade: if I am going to make a complaint to the manager then I need to know what I am talking about, if only to save myself from looking a fool). The more I know the more I want to get involved. To take the fair trade issue again: fair trade depends on fair production, and my concern for fair production may in due course link me with producers in the Third World and thus with world mission. Traditionally our links with mission—I am speaking about Christians in the West—are through missionaries. Concern for fair trade might link us with nationals, an added dimension in our understanding of the world church.

• Start communicating. There has never been a better time. In addition to the faithful letter, there are e-mails, web sites, Facebook, Twitter, cheaper than ever phone calls, radio phone-ins and the like. The importance of advertising, good PR, audience figures, and market research mean that more than ever people want to hear from us, and yet so often Christians are silent. We know very well that the word is powerful (or if not why are we bothering to preach so many sermons?) but you would not guess this from our behaviour. People are writing to us, sending us promotional mail of all sorts, telephoning us (double glazing!) and generally trying to get us to change our minds. It is about time we did something to reverse the flow.

• Set aside specific time. One of the most usual excuses that people make for their inability to help the poor is that they do not have the time. It may be that it will help simply to say that a couple of hours on the weekend or one evening is 'action time'. If the time comes round and you are too busy, well and good, but at least this will have thrown up a marker. It might also help to agree to meet with like-minded friends say once a month, to discuss progress. This may spur us on if only because we do not want to report that there is none!

Another possibility is to give up something that we have been doing previously. Some while ago I decided that I needed to do more serious reading and gave up watching sport on the television for a while in order to achieve this. It was hard work but worth it! On the other hand we do not necessarily have to trade off something which we enjoy. There may well be things that we are doing simply out of habit or duty which we can dispense with. Obviously, everybody must draw up their own list, but here are a few suggestions: clean the house and car less often, go to church only once on a Sunday, avoid unnecessary committee meetings, put outgoings on direct debit and forget about them, stop wasting time to save money (unless you enjoy bargain hunting), check how many times you say after watching a programme on the television 'that was a waste of time' and do something about it, invest in labour saving devices.

I suggest that in all these matters we try the 'what am I going to say to God' technique. Imagine on 'that day' that God says to you: 'now why was it exactly that you never got round to doing something in response to Ezekiel 16:49, even after you read that article...' Your reply is going to have to include some sort of time defence. I was doing something absolutely necessary instead, or something better. Now look at the things that I have suggested you might trade in. Do they really fulfil the criteria? Are they absolutely necessary or obviously better?

Set aside a budget. Have a small amount of money available to finance your programme of social action. You will be surprised how small this sum can be. Using the money is much better than simply giving it away to an organisation to use on your behalf. So if you are really short of cash cancel a subscription to some worthy organisation and appropriate the funds for your campaigning. Only you need to keep accounts with yourself. Put the allocated sum into an envelope or record it in a notebook and sanctify it (i.e. set it aside for God's use only).

We despair of influencing public opinion, but often too quickly. Opinion wars can be won. There is such a thing as public pressure. Public issues, in my experience are subject to 'tipping points'. When I was a youngster drink driving was largely winked at. Not anymore. Over time the issue has become serious. Similarly the facts about smoking and its danger to health have been known for decades. There came a time, however, when people wanted some action. Who would have thought twenty years ago that there would be a ban on smoking in all public places and that this would be happily endorsed by the population at large? Evidently, times do change. Hard times in particular alter the landscape, and it may be that hard times are on the way. Fissures and cracks open up where before there was only a smooth granite wall, and new 'tipping points' emerge. At the very least people may be listening more carefully.

Another way we can 'spread the word' is by giving a voice to people who find it difficult to speak for themselves. I used to teach classes where a majority of the students were from the Global South. They knew that their countries were being exploited by us Westerners but, after all, they had come to the West to further their education and the last thing they wanted to do was to insult their hosts. So they kept quiet. But of course, they had a story to tell, and given the opportunity, or should we say the permission, they were ready to do so. It was a story that we needed to hear because it helped us to see things through others' eyes. It also did our preaching for us more powerfully than we could do it ourselves. So, when last did somebody from the Global South speak in your church? If you are planning to invite someone, get them to talk about issues of poverty and discrimination, of neo-colonialism and globalisation. All sorts of people 'from the margins' could help us by telling us their stories—refugees and asylum seekers, persecuted people from minority religions and cultures, people who have endured war and famine, the victims of big business and big government.

Finally, do we always have to be successful? Sometimes things are worth doing even if we know that we are going to fail. To die trying is better than to live knowing that we never gave it a shot. We need the facts and we need to know what they mean. We need to be willing to get into the action and we need to believe that what we do has a real purpose. We can leave the rest to God.

Reality

What do we mean by 'reality'? Thomas De Zengotita's idea is that reality is the opposite of having unlimited options. (2007, 14) We understand this when we use the phrase 'the reality is...' meaning that despite the appearances we are consigned to something we cannot change. Thus: 'we think that we can choose from a range of jobs now that we have got a degree but *the reality is* that the economic downturn has made graduate jobs difficult to come by'. Or it could be something more straightforward. 'We think that the car has enough petrol but *the reality is* that we are going to run out of fuel before we leave the motorway.'

So when we speak about 'living in context' it is possible that we are fooling ourselves. Reality is harsher than it looks, the choices are fewer. Of course, we are constantly being told that we have choices. 'Where do you want to go today?' says the Microsoft advert. 'Choices for a small world' says Dupont the chemicals firm. 'Just do it!' says Nike, as if it was as easy as that. But the proffered choices are not as real as they seem. Sitting in front of the screen of my computer does not take me wherever I want to go. Dupont's choices may mean the deepening of the environmental crisis that threatens to put an end to all my choices. 'Doing it' the Nike way does not turn me into a fabulously wealthy basketball star, indeed it is infinitely more likely that it will trap me in a sweatshop in some export zone in the Global South.

All this is, perhaps, not very new news. We all know that the mediated world is not, in one sense, the real world, even if we choose to forget this fact on a regular basis. But I am not talking here about the opposite to the fake or plastic. That is certainly one sense of the word, as in 'real' leather which means, we hope, leather that was once the hide of an animal. I am meaning rather a world in which a different sort of supposed reality is on offer, one which has been deliberately constructed to give me a sense that I am being rescued from the old world of limited options.

This new world is the context of most of us in the twenty first century. If you doubt that, try to imagine what your life would be like without a choice in clothes or food or household goods (and the shopping that goes with it), without transport or holidays or leisure pursuits (no entertainment allowed!), without any chance of change of employment or change within your daily occupation, and of course without the media—television, books and papers, cinema and theatre. (I have just described the life of a peasant or forest dweller, certainly until quite recent times.) Most of us would consider this life scarcely human. Yet most of us would also admit that this world of choice which we now enjoy is strangely troubling. People consistently try to 'get away from it'. Religious people go on 'retreats', not generally because they are covert ascetics, but because they are desperate to get away from the manufactured world. They intuitively sense that full blown immersion in the contemporary culture and 'waiting on God' are not compatible.

In Bruce Springsteen's profound little lyric *57 Channels and Nothin' On*[9] he says:

> Now home entertainment was my baby's wish
> So I went into town for a satellite dish
> Tied it to the top of my Japanese car
> Pointed it out into the stars
> Message came back from the great beyond
> Fifty seven channels and nothin' on.

Bruce is frustrated by the lack of good TV programmes, but the real problem—as the rest of the song shows—is that he has everything: huge amounts of money, technology at his beck and call, a girl of his own, and it still adds up to nothing much. He can get what he wants when he wants, choose what he likes, but there's still no message. What Bruce needed to know (and probably did—he's a clever operator) is that he is approaching sanity. When the world of unlimited choice is exhausted, reality takes over, and that can be a good thing.

When I spoke about 'waiting on God' I am not sure that that was the right expression. It is more the need to know that God is there whether we wait on him or not. I used to live up in the mountains in India. I would go outside on a clear night and look at the stars and feel that there was nothing between me and them, in both senses of the expression. They were so near that I could touch them and they were completely indifferent to me. They were just there and would be still there when I was gone and forgotten. I thought (in

9 In Springsteen's album 'Human Touch'(1992).

some moods anyway) that this was better than com-munication.

The great Annie Dillard pointed out that:

> God needs nothing, asks nothing, and demands nothing, like the stars... You do not have to sit outside in the dark. If however, you want to look at the stars, you will find that darkness is necessary. But the stars neither require or demand it.
> (1983, 31)

How do we contextualise the Gospel in this medi-ated culture? Despite what I have been saying about the value of distancing oneself from unreality, of going out from the warmth and light of our rooms into the coldness and stillness of the starlit night: despite this, I do not think that long-term 'flight' is a productive or even possible strategy. As a temporary measure or even an occasional remedy it may be all right, but there should be a limit.

I think this for two reasons. Firstly, we usually take the mediated world with us, or to change the metaphor, unreality is now the oxygen we breathe; it is idle to pretend that we can survive in a different atmosphere. Secondly, I think we are required, to put it very simply, to serve our own generation, even if, to quote the Irishman, to get to our desired destina-tion it would have been easier to have started from somewhere else.

This book is about trying to help us live in context, that is to say to accept reality. But beware! Keeping a grip on reality itself is a struggle. Just think about some of our chapter headings. Take the subject of healing, for example. Most of our prayer for healing is intended to *avoid* reality. (I shall develop this theme in the appropriate chapter.) Or the Bible. A great deal of our use of the Bible is intended to confirm our own choices, rather than challenge them. Again, we have turned 'history' into theme parks, heritage sites and hagiographic biographies, when it should have been 'a negotiation of difficult memory'. (Shanks 2008, 40)

'World' as context

It is obvious that the word 'world' as used in the translations of the New Testament that most of us are reading, has a number of different meanings. To be fair to the Bible translators they are only being faithful to the Greek word *kosmos* which is used in a similarly ambiguous way. So when the author of John's Gospel writes that 'God so loved the world' (3:16) he has one meaning in mind, while the author of 1 John (not necessarily the same person as the evangelist, though he uses the same Greek word) has another when he tells his readers 'do not love the world' (2:15). So in what sense are we using the word when we encourage people to accept 'the world' as their context for life?

The answer is: 'neither of the above'! If I was intending the first sense then I would be saying something so obvious that it would not be worth saying. 'World' in the New Testament can simply mean 'the whole created order'. 'God so loved the world' means that God has a benevolent purpose for the universe. The second meaning is something like 'human society organised against God'. (Walter Wink simply calls it 'the Domination System'.) It is the meaning that we intend when we say that people are 'worldly'. They are living by ungodly standards. If I was intending this meaning then I would be advising Christians to join the opposition.

In my use of the word I want us to think of the world as it actually is, in the sense that it is the context for our actual day-to-day mundane existence. It is not the whole world—just our individual little bit of it; it is not the world organised against God—in fact it contains both good and bad and a good deal in between; it is not the world as we imagine it; it is not the world of yesterday or tomorrow, it is the *real* world, which I encounter whether I like it or not. I can manipulate it to a certain extent, but I will find that it keeps on insisting on its own way, whatever I do. It is simply a massive confusion to think that it is 'spiritual' to live apart from this world, and Christians withdraw from it at their peril.

The confusion is carried forward sometimes by our popular hymns. 'This world is not my home' can easily be misinterpreted; so can the verse in Philippians 3:20 where Paul says that 'our citizenship is in heaven'. Paul is writing to a Roman colony where the privileged settlers had Roman citizenship. They were not therefore living in Rome, nor did they expect to be repatriated to Rome at a later date. Philippi was their home, but at the same time they were living by the standards of Rome, enjoying the privileges of Roman citizenship, and might expect Rome to intervene on their behalf if necessary.

Despite the shallowness of much of our devotional life, Christian people often appear to be more at home among the 'heavenly things' than the 'earthly' ones. This sounds like good news, but there is an important distinction to be made. The language of spirituality: 'meditation', 'quiet times', retreats' and the like, says something good when placed against the busyness which keeps God at a distance; but it says something bad when we create a dualism in which God is *only* found in places of quiet and times of meditation. We have to hear God speak to us about earthly things and that is a condition of hearing the heavenly voice. In terms of our discipleship, for example, it is of no value if we avoid our duty to our neighbour in order to be religious. As Kagawa put it in his *Meditations*:

> God dwells among the lowliest of men. He sits on the dust-heap among the prison convicts. With the juvenile delinquents He stands at the door begging bread. He throngs with the beggars at the place of alms. He is among the sick. He stands in line with the unemployed in front of the free employment bureaus. Therefore let him who would meet God visit the prison cell before going to the temple. Before he goes to church let him visit the hospital. Before he reads the Bible let him help the beggar standing at his door. (Kagawa in Axling 1932, 38)

We have all sorts of ways of maintaining this wrong dualism. There is the 'upstairs, downstairs' approach. God is in his heaven and occasionally he parachutes some help down to us—an answer to prayer, a small miracle—but we actually live on a God-forsaken planet. Or there is the 'here and hereafter' approach. We shall just have to wait and keep our heads down until the weather finally clears up. Jesus was here but (unfortunately) he went away: things will be all right when he comes back. Another form of dualism is spatial. We can find the presence of God, but only in certain designated places—the church building, our home, a deserted and beautiful spot in the countryside. Or, as we have seen, the division is temporal. Certain times belong to God, but not others.

How can we hear God speak about all those troubled areas of our lives that seem far away from Him and which we do not know how to include in any definition of God's rule? Perhaps this was the problem for Nicodemus (as recorded in John chapter 3)[10]. In Jesus the kingdom of God was indeed breaking into what we call 'everyday life', but you had to be 'born again' to see it (verse 5), you had to want it to happen (verse 19) and later on Nicodemus found that there was a cost to pay (John 19:39). (Nicodemus may have guessed this already—see the reference in verse 2 to a visit by night.) Much of the protracted debate on whether the preaching of the Gospel comes first and social concern comes second (or vice versa) might benefit from this passage. The question which lay behind Nicodemus's opening comment (verse 2) was 'Where is God truly at work today?' (Mark's equivalent question is: 'How shall we describe the kingdom of

10 The substance of the following remarks on John chapter 3 originally appeared in the Commentary series in *Third Way* March 2007.

God?') The answer he got was that the action of God's Spirit is as uncontrollable as the wind. It is not confined to a place or a time or a method. It is certainly not confined to the realms of heaven. It is as if Jesus is saying, 'Nicodemus, there are all sorts of rumours ("you hear the sound of it") that God is doing a new thing, and they are true rumours. The trouble with you is that you want to rush on to heavenly things when you have not yet received the earthly things that will tell you what you need to know.'

I suspect that one of the reasons why we are often suspicious of Christian social action, for example, is that God's presence there seems like a rumour that is difficult to verify in the usual way. The people involved are not 'our people', the places are not 'our places'; God is not given the credit often enough and the end product is not exactly what we had hoped for. Above all we are not really in control of the process—and God, we think, needs *us* to control things. Is it because he is worried about losing control that Nicodemus is gently teased by Jesus about being a teacher (verse 9)?

'Believing is seeing' says Jesus (verse 21). It is we Christians who are often trapped in unbelief. We have crafted our own version of the kingdom and cannot believe that there might be another one. We need to allow the wind of the Spirit to blow into our minds so that we can see the light that has come , and is still coming, into the world.

Contextualisation

Here, I think it would be worth putting in a brief word about the theory of contextualisation. The reader will deduce (correctly) from what I have already written that I believe that there is a real world. I am not, for example, somebody who thinks that what Peter Berger calls 'the social construction of reality' is the whole story. On the other hand I am not a foundationalist either. I do not think that encountering the real world or 'knowing the truth of the matter' is straightforward. The simple question, 'how do we know what we know?' throws up a very complex answer. Language is 'constructed' ('when I use a word it means what I want it to mean' said Humpty Dumpty), customs and cultures 'colour' the way we see things, our inadequate knowledge creates multiple misunderstandings, our prejudices 'block off' conclusions that we would have reached if we had considered the matter fairly. Does that mean that we never encounter reality, that living in context is actually impossible? Clearly it is difficult, but not so difficult that we have to despair. The challenge is to *work* at it. We may never be fully in the light, but the darkness is not absolute either. As in so many matters, we must not quit trying to be humans because we are not God.

The truth is that we simply cannot go back to the old style confidence in absolutes particularly the claim by Westerners that they are the product of Christian civilisation. For a variety of (good) reasons we have moved on from this position and ethnocentricity's successor, contextualization, however we define it, seems the better way. Yet there is a debate here.

The move to contextualization is just part of a wider shift in epistemology (the way we know what we know). The worldview characterised by claims to the knowledge of 'absolute truths' has been superseded by epistemological provisionality whereby truths are necessarily embedded in a particular culture and mediated to us through a particular worldview. While not all truth claims are equally valid and greater objectivity is a possibility, our knowledge is nevertheless provisional, real but incomplete. This shift of perspective holds good for our apprehension of the truths of Scripture as much as for any other truths. They are mediated to us through a culture, which has to be studied and understood. Our interpretation of Scripture is subject to the same limitations—provisionality, incompleteness—which I have mentioned above. Again this does not mean that we see no truth. 'We see through a glass darkly, but we do see', and furthermore we may reasonably claim that some truths are clearer than others.

While we have to take culture seriously, we also need to remember that recent anthropological theory has tended to extreme cultural relativism. Anthropologists of a certain era and a certain school wanted us to believe that you could not communicate accurately across cultures. Not many people nowadays think that the situation is as dire as that. Having said this, something approaching a new attitude to discerning the truth may indeed be necessary, when we try to confront someone else's culture. Instead of replacing his or her 'truth' by my 'truth', there will need to be a joint search. In this the basic skill becomes that of interpretation rather than legislation, aiming less at 'knowledge' and more at 'understanding'.

We need to understand afresh (what I think we have always known) that the proclamation of the Gospel is not a matter of proclaiming 'absolute truths', but rather the person of Christ. The Gospel is 'the good news of Jesus Christ' (Mark 1:1). In the same way that we get to know another culture best, not by reading about it in a book, but by relating personally to people in that culture, so 'getting to know Jesus' is the best starting place for people from within a culture who have not previously encountered the Gospel. Similarly, we must treat the Bible not as a source book for universal truths but as the authentic witness to Jesus. Having encountered Jesus, people can be encouraged to read the Bible 'through the eyes of Jesus' so to speak, what the scholars call 'a Christocentric hermeneutic'. Indeed we can take this even further. We also need a 'logos theology' (John 1:1-4) in which Christ is discovered not only in the Bible but in the experience (and culture) of the local community.

What does all this mean for the practice of contextualisation? Here are some points.

• Care must be taken to interpret the Bible in an honest way, using the scholarly disciplines where appropriate. Too often our approach to Biblical interpretation is no more than a means of preferring our own culture over that of others.

• The careful study of cultures—our own and others'—with a view to greater understanding, remains essential. Contextualisation involves commitment. There are no short cuts.

• The church (i.e., the local church) is the appropriate hermeneutic community. Contextualisation is not a job for 'experts' but for the people of God. It is the ongoing process by which the church struggles to discover what it means to confess Jesus as Lord in its changing context.

• Dialogue becomes an essential tool. We need to learn to listen to people just as much as we need to tell them about the good news. Apart from anything else this can clear up misunderstandings. Syncretism—the retention of elements of thought and behaviour which are incompatible with the confession of Jesus Christ as Lord—is likely to result, often as an unacknowledged or secret process, from lack of dialogue.

In practice most contexts display considerable cultural diversity. A church may find that its 'one size fits all' services do not meet the need of its mixed congregation. Creating a church which is welcoming, for example, to people who have little previous experience of a church culture, may prove costly. This may be part of the well-known choice between 'mission and maintenance'; effective mission is almost always costly in this way. (Ingleby 1997)

When we speak of 'contextualisation' we also have to take into account that we live in an increasingly postmodern and postcolonial world. R. S. Surgirtharajah thinks that we have had enough talk about contextualisation, describing it as an 'exhausted model'. 'All around us there is a hermeneutical fatigue, and a feeling that we have heard all these things before.' But he is not asking for another 'grand narrative', rather a greater understanding of, and adaption to, an increasingly varied and hybrid world. (Surgirtharajah 2002, 122-5 .)

THE CONTEXT OF CONTEMPORARY CULTURE

What I want to do in this section is to look at some of the really big movements of our time—so big that, because they lie beyond our day-to-day focus on events, we often ignore them. Yet they are truly our inescapable context and affect our lives in profound ways.

Globalisation

The trouble with globalisation as a process is that it seems too big to handle. It is one of those vague, threatening realities which we have no choice but to leave others to deal with—if they can. We have enough difficulty influencing our immediate context—family, workplace, church, neighbourhood—without pretending that we can do much about the wider world. Yet this is to ignore something very powerful that is increasingly bearing down upon us and changing our lives dramatically. If we are truly to understand our lives then we must realise that they are placed within this context too.

I see globalisation, in its contemporary manifestation, as very much the enemy, indeed as the prelude to some sort of baleful apocalypse. I am not alone in this. I stand with a number of Christian writers such as Timothy Gorringe, Ched Myers and Wendell Berry, as well as commentators from a variety of academic disciplines, most notably the environmentalists, who share this concern. My own feeling is that we *underestimate* the threat. We need language which is more confrontational, more violent, to describe what is happening. Let me give you just one example. Ziauddin Sardar and Meryl Wyn Davies, in their book *Why Do People Hate America?* try very hard to explain to Westerners, and to Americans in particular, why it is that people are so troubled by globalisation. I hope they succeed but I am not sure that people are listening. Take their fourth chapter, 'American Hamburgers and Other Viruses'. What's wrong with hamburgers, anyway, we ask, and are quite happy to crowd into McDonald's and other American fast food outlets. All we are doing, we say, is taking advantage of a cheap and readily available meal served in a familiar setting. Well, that is one way of putting it. Our authors put it this way:

> The tsunami of American consumerist culture assimilates everything, exerting immense, unstoppable pressure on the people of much of the world to change their lifestyles, to abandon all that gives meaning to their lives, to throw away not just their values but also their identity, stable relationships, attachment to history, buildings, places, families and received ways of doing and being.
> (Sardar & Davies 2002, 121)

Surely, we say, that language is much too dramatic? We were talking about harmless hamburgers and along come these people and transmute them into a dangerous virus! But what about the overall effects of rapid cultural change in our world? Have we ever stopped to think about its possible consequences? It is certainly true that everywhere we go we see the wreckage of what were once vibrant and life sustaining cultures; we see this, but we do not know how to account for it. As Christian people we try as best we can to help. Perhaps we feel responsibility for the 100 million[11] plus street children. Brave souls go and live and work in the urban slums of Sao Paulo, Manila, Mumbai, Nairobi and the like. But how did all these needy people get there in the first place? Where did they come from? Why have they abandoned their ways of life which served them well for centuries? Is this really 'the better life' or has Western consumerism promised one thing and delivered another? And where does the church come into it?

If you look up 'Anti-globalisation' web sites you will find that what is meant by globalisation is usually *economic* globalisation. Those who are against globalisation in this way are often expressing their opposition to new forms of capitalism. One of the questions that globalisation raises is whether, in terms of economics, we are really into something genuinely new or whether it is simply that capitalism has greater opportunities than previously.

Manuel Castells, for one, thinks that capitalism is changing in a radical way and that it has effectively been restructured in recent decades, both as a result of globalisation and as a contribution to it (Castells 2000, 1-2). He mentions some key developments. There has been a great deal of decentralisation lead-

11 This is the UNICEF estimate (2002). It is agreed, however, that it is difficult to be conclusive about the numbers involved; much depends on the definition of the term.

ing to patterns of networking (Castells's key word). The old division of labour and capital is still there but the balance seems to have swung in favour of capital. In fact many feel that the labour movement, as such, is in terminal decline.

This is partly because people are working in different ways. The labour force is more diversified with more individual work patterns. The greater number of women in the workforce has accentuated this trend. Due to a number of pressures—political, economic and ideological—the state is playing a less active role in the economic life of nations. There is increased global competition (nations find that competitors can come from anywhere) and this has been aided by the global integration of the financial markets. Taken together these developments have produced a world in which the most valuable economic segments work increasingly as a unit. These are then able to maximise their advantage against the rest. Hence uneven economic development is more than ever a feature of a globalising world. (Christians need to realise that the relatively bland phrase 'uneven economic development' means that there is a greater than ever gap between the rich and the poor.)

In geopolitical terms we now have the following relatively new situations. The US remains the greatest economic force, but it is rapidly being overtaken by nations such as China and India, with the Asian Pacific region increasingly becoming the new global manufacturing centre. Economic unification has allowed (Western) Europe to remain a major economic power; by contrast we see the increasing marginalisation of some parts of the Global South (especially, but not exclusively, sub-Saharan Africa) as an economic force, and the transformation of Russia and the former Soviet territories into relatively weak market economies. All of these developments should be of interest to Christian people and will, for example, have a bearing on the success of our mission enterprises.

Finally whether we see it as part of capitalism or not, criminal activities have become global, not to mention highly profitable. This is a development which is sometimes called *perverse integration*, and which leads both to social exclusion for some and to the growth of a group which has chosen a profitable, if risky, way to make a living. Sadly, perverse integration seems to be a more and more powerful trend. It may be that a growing underworld is becoming an essential feature of society world-wide (Held & McGrew 2000, 348-54). Many of our Christian ministries will be involved in dealing with the fall-out from these criminal activities.

One further point. Castells not only believes that major changes have taken place recently but suggests that change is here to stay. Information technology will continue to dominate our lives, will be even more productive, and will power the global economy, though the sharing of the newly created wealth will remain problematic and some territories and people will remain 'switched-off'. Those who feel themselves excluded may increasingly resort to violence. The nation state will survive, but on one hand local and regional arrangements will proliferate, and on the other the global economy and geopolitics will be managed by multilateral institutions and international security alliances. Global security will be a rising concern with tensions in the Pacific, the resurgence of Russia, and international terrorism. People will be yet more alienated from the sources of power. We can look forward to 'informed bewilderment' (Castells 1998, 389) Not a happy picture!

All this may seem, as I have said, rather remote, but there is one very familiar aspect of globalisation, namely the growth of businesses which have a global reach. These companies, often called Trans National Corporations (TNCs), affect all our lives. We may not know much about globalisation in a theoretical sense, but we have seen Starbucks appear on our High Street, bought GAP and NIKE products, eaten at McDonald's and written our documents on a word-processing package marketed by Microsoft.

Typically, TNCs do not mind *where* they produce, as long as it gives them a competitive edge, and they will distribute worldwide if they can. TNCs can be very large indeed and their number is increasing. Taken together, they already control almost one third of the world's total economic output and account for three-quarters of world trade. All this raises some very important questions to do with accountability to the community. If a TNC can be so powerful, and involved in so many aspects of our lives, who controls it?

Some have suggested that directors of big companies are responsible to their shareholders in the same way that governments are responsible to their citizens. However the relationship of investor to company is not at all similar to that of citizen to nation. Normally shareholders have little responsibility in the running of a company and indeed are not much interested, as long as they are getting a reasonable return on their investment. Citizens, on the other hand, do have responsibilities to the state and these go far beyond economic returns. It is quite wrong to think of citizenship purely in consumer terms, with the state's only role to provide us with goods and services in return for our taxes. The state makes legitimate demands on us in many areas such as defence (conscription), law and order (jury service), upkeep of the environment (laws against pollution). In some countries, like Australia, citizen responsibility is underlined by making voting a compulsory civic duty.

Also, we rightly feel responsible for the control of our governments even when we feel they are largely out of control. We hold our leaders responsible. We believe that they should set an example and be above reproach. A President of the United States can be impeached for trying to cover up actions which are thought to be immoral. The Chairman of a Board of Directors faces no such danger, unless the misdemeanour has to do with the financial effectiveness of the corporation. I feel ashamed at some of my government's policies, even when it is not the government of my choice. You might argue that shareholders are equally ashamed when they find out that the company in which they have invested is using, for example, exploitive labour practices. Possibly, but it is hardly analogous. The most drastic action we are likely to take is to disinvest. But we cannot opt out of our national identity. This shows how unlike the two situations are.

In brief, TNCs lack democratic control and accountability. As Jonathan Freedman has put it, there is 'a shift from representativity to manageability'. Government itself is in danger of becoming less about political projects and ideologies and more about efficient management. It is the sort of government, all too familiar to us today, which relies on the opinions of advisers and lobbyists, rather than the democratic process. TNCs, particularly banded together in what Freedman calls 'transnational discourse communities', (the sort of community that sends its chief men to the Davos Forum every year) indirectly provide us with a new sort of political leadership, a supposedly wise transnational elite which knows better than the people what the people need and want (Freedman 2002, 140-1). This faith has been shaken recently, but despite the evident failures displayed in the economic crash post 2008 I think we are still believers. For example, we are waiting for the banks to 'get back to profitability' rather than making a serious attempt to hold them to account for their part in the disaster.

If TNCs and the like are playing an increasing role in our society this has to be addressed, particularly if we feel that their practices are unfair. We agonise, rightly, over any suggestion that our political process is becoming less democratic, yet democracy may be slipping away because of developments on the economic front. One of the alarming things about economic globalisation is that, apparently, winners and losers cease to sit at the same table. In the old order employers and workers may have been unequal in status but at least they needed each other. A workmen's strike could be a devastating tool precisely because the employer could not carry on his business without his workforce. Globalisation, by contrast, can apparently pass by whole populations who never become in any way necessary to production of goods, though they may be important as consumers. Even here they need to have money in their pockets if they are going to have any influence. People are being introduced to the ideas of freedom and choice, but not enjoying its fruits.

Arundhati Roy eloquently laments these huge divisions in society:

> As Indian citizens, we subsist on a regular diet of caste massacres and nuclear tests, mosque breaking and fashion shows, church burning and expanding cell phone networks, bonded labour and the digital revolution, female infanticide and the Nasdaq crash, husbands who continue to burn their wives for dowry, and our delectable stockpile of Miss Worlds. I don't mean to put a simplistic value judgement on this particular form of 'progress' by suggesting that Modern is Good and Traditional is Bad—or vice versa. What's hard to reconcile oneself to, both personally and politically, is the schizophrenic nature of it. In the lane behind my house, every night I walk past road-gangs of emaciated labourers digging a trench to lay fibre-optic cables to speed up our digital revolution. In the bitter winter cold, they work by the light of a few candles. [Roy 2002,168]

John Comaroff gives another description, this time from South Africa.

> Simultaneous possibilities and impossibilities. For young blacks in South Africa that is the situation. No regular employment, no steady income, no security, no basis on which to create a family or an adult life, no tomorrow. Yet, at the same time, they do not have to look far to see 'new' business people making fortunes very quickly. Images of easy wealth also come to them through the media. They are aware of space-time compression by which people, objects, information and currency move without any visible effort but with value added. (Goldberg 2002, 35).

And a final comment from Peter Beilharz.

> The 'gated cities' and the 'no-go' areas go together. What we call the public sphere tends to disappear in the middle. It is not just that we disagree, there is no meeting place anymore (Beilharz 2000, 155).

Strangely, despite the (successful) attempts of rich and powerful people to disconnect their enterprises from the needs of the poor, at another level, uneven economic development now increasingly stares them in the face. Because of our newly found global consciousness it is more difficult than ever for the wealthy to ignore the poor. We may not want to do much about it but at least we know that people in Mozambique and North Korea and Afghanistan are starving. In any case one surprising aspect of globalisation is that the so-called Third World, once somewhere you had to travel to from the wealthy world, is now everywhere. (Wealthy cities like London, Paris and New York have always had poor people living in them, but the phenomenon of rich and poor in close proximity is increasingly part of the globalised world.) This is partly because of the world wide movement of populations and also because of the growing gap between the rich and the poor.

The way that our world cities can demonstrate such stark contrasts is something which alerts people today to disparities of wealth and makes it more difficult for them to take an 'us and them' attitude to other cultures and communities. It may also fuel conflict and violence. Critics of this description suggest that there is evidence that the middle class is growing in a healthy way in many countries. India might be an example. This would give us three groupings: elites, contented and marginalised. Critics of the critics would want to add that globalisation has increased the wealth of elites in a dramatic fashion, done a little for the contented, but made the marginalised more than ever desperate.

Behind the debate on poverty is the critical question of causation. For example, you often hear it said that poverty is the result of being cut off from the 'flow' of world capital, from globalisation, which just proves that globalisation is a good thing. There is some truth in this, but as a statement it is largely tautologous. Poverty has always been caused by some people having money and others being excluded.

What needs to be examined is how and why this happens and how it can be changed. If people have to accept unfair wages simply because they are starving and nobody will pay them enough to live on, and if this is a widespread situation, then this requires our attention and the sort of attention required has to do with what we call politics.

The point is surely that those with power have always used their power to exploit those who are weak and that some positive action has to be taken to put this right. People are cut off from the global market because others have got there first. That is the story of history. We have always had 'robber barons' who have used their power to live in comparative luxury at the expense of an impoverished countryside. (We have them today. They are called Trans National Corporations.) Of course they did some good. The baron's establishment provided some employment, no doubt, but the *basis* of his wealth was exploitive taxation backed by force. Wealthy landowners during the industrial revolution simply exploited the workers in their mines and mills instead of the peasants. Globalisation means that it is happening still, but on a bigger scale. The wealthy nations are networked today to their own profit. The TNCs hardly need the umbrella of nations at all. Both will have to be *forced* to make their wealth work for the poorer parts of the world, if there is to be significant change. There is little evidence that that is happening. The system is rigged.

> A thin segment of the super rich...has formed a stateless alliance that defines *global interest* as synonymous with the personal and corporate financial interests of its members
>
> (Goldsmith 2001, 39)

Workers in the developing world cannot sell their labour at a fair price and the Common Agricultural Policy subsidises European agriculture at the expense of poorer nations—just to take two examples. The wealthy are simply not willing to cut in the poorer nations on the deal.

A word here about trade. Trade, we are told, is the appropriate response to 'comparative advantage'. Different parts of the world find it easier to produce different commodities. They should be allowed to exploit the advantage this gives them and exchange what they have with others who are exploiting theirs. Thereby everybody wins. This should produce a 'bigger cake' and a bigger cake could mean more for everyone. Furthermore, choice is good. Who wants to be stuck with bread and water when you can have cheese and wine as well.

There are some snags, however. There are obvious advantages in local communities producing what they need to survive, before they start thinking about what they can exchange. Cash crops for sale abroad are not always what a community needs in order to be secure. Flowers may be more exchangeable, but less edible than maize or wheat. Schaeffer's comment on agricultural change is salutary.

> The Green Revolution has both increased the volume of world food supplies but at the same time displaced small farmers and reduced the production of staple foods. Both developments contribute to hunger
> (Schaeffer 2003, 180)

Trade can also have environmental costs. World-wide swapping means world-wide transport systems with their pollutive effects.

Then you have the balance between free and fair trade. Free traders have argued that 'the market knows best'; governments which regulate in the name of security stifle initiative and lead to inefficiency and corruption. Fair traders argue on the other side that trade is always conducted according to rules, what you have to do is to ensure that they are the right rules. When the rules are drawn up by the rich nations and in favour of the big players, this is the opposite of 'a level playing field'.

> How can local support alone enable small producers and locally owned shops to flourish if corporate welfare and free trade policies heavily promote the interests of large-scale producers and marketers?
> (Goldsmith 2001, 245)

Perhaps, as fair traders say, there is something to be said for 'protection', when you live in the jungle. In any case how free is 'free' trade? As Robert Schaeffer has commented about the sort of 'free trade' we have experienced up to now:

> In many cases free trade agreements opened markets not to competition between businesses but to monopoly because they facilitated the entry of large-scale multinationals. (Schaeffer 2003, 238)

One of the great indictments against globalisation is that it has pinned its hopes on economic growth as a universal panacea. Growth in fact is an obsession in our world, and has too often been seen as the *only* sign of health. 'I know that my company, my mission, my college is in good shape because it is growing.' Much the same thing is being said about churches!

Some very obvious questions immediately arise, however. What sort of growth? Who is measuring it? Who is benefiting from it? Can it be sustained? Is it at the expense of other sorts of growth? 'Growth', used as an all purpose term, is a close acquaintance of our old friend 'progress', so beloved by the Enlightenment, but without the same sense of the future. The Enlightenment had a strong sense of 'project', of improving the world by rational means, but 'growth', particularly economic growth, often means little more than making more money than we did before. Also, 'growth' as currently experienced does not have any element of distributive justice included in it. The argument that the bigger pie means bigger portions all round is clearly true only if the extra pie is available for distribution!

Also, what are the ingredients of the pie? Worryingly, the rich may be making a bigger pie but the additional ingredients have been stolen from the poor, or by using up non-renewable natural resources, stolen from future generations. Are we really convinced that first world affluence has nothing to do with the poverty of the developing world? As Jeremy Seabrook has put it:

> Poverty cannot be "cured", for it is not a symptom of the disease of capitalism. Quite the reverse: it is evidence of its robust good health, its spur to even greater accumulation and effort. (Seabrook in Beilharz 2000, 158)

There is much debate at the present time as to whether the world has become a better place to live over the past few decades. There are those who claim that the last twenty years of the world's history has experienced unprecedented success in the raising of living standards. Though it may be that in some cases the gap between rich and poor has widened, they say, the important point is that the poor are less poor than they used to be. I am not sure that this case in itself is proven. George Monbiot's article in the *Guardian* (May 26, 2003) 'Poor, but Pedicured' under the heading 'It appears that those at the bottom are getting richer—but sadly the maths just doesn't add up', suggests that recent research by Sanjay Reddy and Thomas Pogge throw much doubt on the World Bank's figures that are supposed to 'prove' that the poor are indeed better off.

It is always difficult to know the rights and the wrongs of the statistical battle, but it is significant that, nearer to home, the investigative journalists Barbara Ehrenreich (in the States) and Polly Toynbee (in the UK) both report that it is now harder than ever for those who work on the minimum wage to keep their heads above water economically. (See Ehrenreich 2002 and Toynbee 2003.) If the 'poor are getting poorer' in the affluent world (and we know that in the case of many countries in the global South there is a transference of wealth from poorer economies to richer) then it seems unlikely that those beneath the poverty line in places like Kenya or Moldova or Indonesia are really improving their economic status. I suspect that *in absolute terms* the poor have recently been in even greater difficulties than usual: the effects of global warming and environmental disasters, the AIDS epidemic, the determination of the wealthy West to restructure developing economies in a way that makes them vulnerable to aggressive capitalism, the falling price on the world market of some primary commodities and the corruption of governments are just some of the reasons that have been suggested.

It is possible to argue about the items on this list individually, but it is difficult, for all that, not to feel that overall something has gone badly wrong and that the poor are increasingly the losers in the 'global game'. Have we in all this been borrowing from the future? Are we using up scarce resources with no accounting for what future generations may need? We should remind ourselves of Simone Weil's comment:

> There is no reason at all why in trying to make the conditions of production furnish a greater yield they must always be developed. One can just as easily exhaust them.
> (Weil 2001, 177)

Similarly 'living as if there were no tomorrow' has a sinister ring about it nowadays, particularly if you are an environmentalist. We also need to ask whose tomorrow we are talking about. The 1998 UNDP report claims that 86 per cent of global consumption takes place among 20 per cent of the total global population. As Crystal Bartolovich points out: A child born in the industrial world 'adds more to consumption and pollution over his or her lifetime than do 30-50 children born in the developing world' (Bartolovich 2003, 181).

In other words, the global North is currently using up by far the larger part of the world's resources: is the South prepared to accept this situation? If not, then either the North will have to share some of its resources or accept that the growing demand in the South will tip the world even more sharply towards ecological disaster. Also towards conflict: as Bartolovich adds:

> Since it is literally impossible for all the world to consume at the level of the 'advanced' capitalisms, the Northern nations must be kept as gated communities (which, as we all know, open the gates for maids, gardeners and provisions, as well as residents).
> (Bartolovich 2003, 183)

Though the idea of economic growth appears to have an orientation towards the future, an 'agenda for the planet' as DuPont advertising has it, I very much doubt the reality. The profit motive increasingly dictates a short-term strategy. Unless my company can be seen to be making substantial profits now, or appears to be about to make them in the very near future, it will easily fall prey to its rivals, who are promising shareholders quick returns. Notice also the huge levels of debt that are being sustained today in all sorts of contexts. This is true of the most 'successful' countries such as Japan and the United States, as well as the poor nations. Debt used to mean that I was borrowing against the future so that I could spend now. In fact, that is what it still does mean. People in poor nations, say in sub-Saharan Africa, have borrowed so heavily that they can no longer afford adequate health services. 'Eat, drink, and be merry for tomorrow we die.' The truth is that our ancestors often invested very heavily in the future (and we are living in the good of it) because they believed in it. But we do not, so why bother?

Is the growth of, say, the last twenty years (about the time people began to speak of globalisation) based on practices that will in due course systematically remove the protection previously afforded to the poor against the rapacious rich? For example, is globalisation eroding the power of the state to protect its own citizens. I think history helps us here.

The long nineteenth century in Britain (1789-1914) saw not only the growth of industrial capitalism, but also a concerted attempt by the government through social legislation such as mines and factory acts, the legalisation of trade unions, state insurance, progressive taxation and the like, to protect those without capital from those with financial and property power. Notice that this was not done by philanthropy or self regulation but by state intervention. This was partially successful. In the twentieth century the Liberal government of 1906-14 laid the foundations of the welfare state introducing taxation on land and wealth to finance insurance and pensions for the poor.[12]

Another attempt was made in 1945-51 by the Labour Government to take the principle further. This was done in the light of the failures of capitalism in the twenties and thirties ('The Great Slump'). The result was a substantial equalisation of wealth and a nation in which, on the whole, the populace could count on warm clothes, food on the table and a roof over their heads. (Of course there were still great inequalities.) This is the merest sketch, but it illustrates a substantial point and raises an important question. Who will protect us if globalisation subverts the powers of the state?

The reason why we have states, especially democratic states, is that we need umpires and arbiters. Thomas Hobbes saw this, and wrote about it eloquently in his book *Leviathan*. Hobbes lived during the period of the English Civil War and, like many of his contemporaries, saw strong government as the only answer to threatening societal chaos. In our day too, it is not difficult to agree with him that there has

12 Lloyd George's People's Budget... 'changed the whole basis of British public finance from the Victorian pattern to the system that has lasted throughout the twentieth century. It shifted the chief source of revenue from indirect to direct taxation; it established the principle that taxation ought to be related to the capacity to pay and it inaugurated a limited redistribution of income for the benefit of the poor through social welfare schemes'. (Pugh 1988, 47)

never been a just society without some sort of agreed human government. That is why Paul commends the idea of government in Romans 13. Paul does not think, after all, that 'Caesar is Lord' but rather that the institution of government itself is 'ordained of God' (verse 1). Globalisation reverts to 'the law of the jungle', in the sense that those who are powerful economically, usually but not entirely trans-national corporations, are given the freedom to roam the jungle at will 'seeking whom they may devour'.

In what ways does the state need to intervene? Based largely but not entirely on the experience of Asian economies in recent times, we can fairly confidently claim the following:

- Ordinary people need to own the land. They will not get it unless the government makes sure that they get it through government intervention in the land market.

- Education (presumably provided by governments) is crucial. Government must intervene in this area too.

- A fair minimum wage is an essential not a luxury

- Better working conditions create greater productivity and must be government guaranteed. A good inspectorate for example is essential.

- Monopolies are bad and should be legislated against. The American anti-trust legislation is an example of this.

- Trade needs to be fair.

- There is a strong case for selective regulation.

This last point needs further comment. Historically, Britain, Germany, the USA., Japan, India, China all *began* with regulation (trade barriers etc.) and then deregulated when they were in a strong enough position to do so and not be swamped by their rivals. The success of the Asian Tigers is often held up as a prime example of successful deregulation. It should be noted however that the Asian Tigers attended to a number of matters first, for example more equitable social arrangements and in some cases land re-distribution. When the time came to go for growth they continued to show preference for domestic companies and to provide some protection from foreign ones. The state never ceased to play an active role in the economy.

Furthermore, many of the prosperous Western countries—Britain, France, Germany, the Scandinavian countries etc.—have experienced a good deal of welfare state socialism during the same period in which they were becoming successful trading countries. Wealth was not only created, it was also distributed. On the other side of the fence, North Korea and Cuba have been held up as examples of nations that have been impoverished because they have not 'opened up' to world trade. There is obviously some truth in this, but particularly in the case of Cuba, there were other international factors which made growth exceedingly difficult. Cuba was willing to trade (on its own terms) but was not allowed to do so. Another example of un-free trade. North Korea's policy has not been one of selected protectionism but of complete isolationism, a very different matter.

In brief, selected regulation by means of state intervention deserves a better press. Even the British government's White Paper on International Development concedes 'it is not inevitable that globalisation will work for the poor—nor that it works against them. This depends on the policies that governments and international agencies pursue'[13]. Free trade and protectionism need not be treated as opposites. While it is true that liberalisation does sometimes help the poor, the fundamental question is what sort of trade? (A good description of the sort of rules that we need to govern world trade is provided in Mark Curtis's book, *Trade for Life: Making Trade Work for Poor People* (Curtis 2001)).

One example from history: during the second half of the nineteenth century there were very serious famines in India. Why was this? Mike Davis has written a compelling book to try and answer this question. He shows how an unprotected market could bring disaster to local producers who had previously coped reasonably well with hard times. He comments:

> There is persuasive evidence that peasants and farm labourers became dramatically more pregnable to natural disaster after 1850 as their local economies were violently incorporated into the world market.
> (Davis 2001, 288)

He gives the following commentary. First of all small hold production was forcibly incorporated into

13 *Eliminating World Poverty: Making Globalisation Work for the Poor* London, The Stationery Office, 2000, 19

commercial systems controlled from overseas. Concurrent with the integration of tropical cultivators into the world system, however, there was a fall in their terms of trade. There was no attempt to rescue the farmers from their dilemma as this would have 'distorted' the 'free' market. Finally, more obvious aspects of imperialism undermined local autonomy and prevented local responses to the crisis. This may seem rather remote from our situation today and rather technical, but I mention it because it is an example of British imperialism (so, for a change, I am not attacking the IMF) and also because British *Christian* imperialism was at its zenith—the idea that Britain had been given India in order to 'bless' her—but that did not seem to make any difference.

Despite the fear of government intervention the evidence seems to suggest that what we need is more (good) government—a better gardener for the garden, not a jungle. Even capitalism needs this. As Arundhati Roy amusingly puts it:

> If we have the right institutions of governance in place—effective courts, good laws, honest politicians, participatory democracy, a transparent administration that respects human rights and gives people a say in decisions that affect their lives—then the globalisation project will work for the poor as well. They call this 'globalisation with a human face'. The point is, if all this was in place anything would succeed: socialism, capitalism, you name it. Everything works in Paradise.
> (Roy 2002, 181-2).

But we do not have Paradise; what we have is an era of insecure employment. One of the certainties of post-Fordism and 'flexible labour' (economic globalisation) is that the era of secure *employment* is over. The reasons usually given are that we have more demanding consumers (choice!), there is more global competition, and more rapid technological change. Whatever the reasons, more workers than ever are employed on a temporary or casual basis, there is little job security and fewer long-term benefits. Also the actual employment pattern of organisations has changed. Firms tend to operate with a small core of permanent staff and an 'outer circle' of casual, part-time, seasonal or home workers (Cohen & Kennedy 2000, 72).

The results of this process are all around us. There is a world-wide search by the bigger corporations for local skills and cheap labour. The location of industrial plant is largely determined by considerations of profitably judged on a world-wide basis. De-industrialisation is therefore as common as industrialisation. Many areas, such as the 'rustbelt' zones in the United States, with high labour costs and obsolete equipment are simply not able to compete in a post-Fordist world. In some cases this applies to whole nations.

As if this were not enough John Gray links terrorism to economic globalisation as well. The link, he suggests, is a failed capitalism. For example, plans to re-make Middle Eastern economies on a Western economic model are bound to fail—with a predictable backlash. More generally he considers that efforts to restructure the world economy on a free market model are not sustainable and will only raise false expectations. He cites the deflation in Japan and the huge amount of American debt as current indicators. He is concerned that worldwide economic integration may be a curse rather than a blessing, producing 'a synchronised global collapse'.[14]

'If national free markets have known violent fluctuations, why not the global one?' he asks. He adds, in a powerful phrase:

> Globalisation is only the entropic drift of technology, interacting unpredictably with divergent cultures and primordial human needs. (Gray 2002, 52-3)

According to Anthony Giddens, insecurity in employment is just one aspect of a society newly characterised by *risk*. He distinguishes external risk which comes from the outside, from the fixities of tradition and nature, and manufactured risk which refers to situations which we have very little historical experience of confronting, because we have created them ourselves (e.g. global warming). Manufactured risks are hugely on the increase as a result of globalisation.

Nor is this just a matter of, for example, environmental disasters. If institutions, as such, are becoming more uncertain, as in the case of marriage, then risk increases. Also, manufactured risk defies calculation (a nightmare for insurers) because we simply do not know what the level of risk is. Global warming is again a good example (Giddens 1999, 28-9). In summary,

14 Gray wrote this in 2002. Events in 2008 proved him right. He was ,however, trying to issue a warning about capitalism in general which seems to have been largely ignored.

> Living in a global age means coping with a
> diversity of new situations of risk. (35)

What creates the sense of an even deeper insecurity than Giddens' risk perhaps, is the way that globalisation has called into question certain longstanding political assumptions, what Frans Schuurman calls 'controlling beliefs' (Schuurman 2001, 4-14).

Schuurman identifies three of these. Firstly there was the essential difference between the First (developed) and the Third (developing) world; secondly an unconditional belief in progress and the possibility of constructing society, and thirdly the importance of the nation state in the realisation of progress.

This may not seem all that dramatic, but imagine for a moment that you are losing faith, as Schuurman suggests we are, in this trio of propositions. In the first place, all those people 'out there' whom we once believed lived in a different world from us, the Third World, are, or should be, free to join us on equal terms; we have to replace the whole idea of inequality with the concept of diversity. Quite a thought! (I develop this a little further under the heading of Postmodernism.)

Secondly, suppose we have given up on Progress. We have decided that we do not know that the future will in fact be better than the past. What have we got left? I suppose little remains but Giddens' world of risk and that to an infinite degree.

Or finally, what if it is true that we can no longer rely on the nation state to lead us into the future or even protect us? We have already seen how insecure that makes us. Who will protect us if the state is unwilling or unable to do so?

Schuurman himself, I judge, is rather alarmed by this new way of thinking. He hints that we are in danger of 'throwing away the baby with the bathwater'. Do we really want to lose the idea of inequality? Westerners may be happy with this (I doubt it) but is the Global South?

> I have the strong impression...that the majority of peasants and people in the South are really interested in getting the right price for their products, and having access to bilingual education, electricity, transportation, and adequate health care. (Schuurman 2001, 10).

Also he wonders whether the Global South is ready to abandon the idea of Progress. Risk, the apparent alternative, is something that we in the First World have created. Is it really all right for us to emphasise these risks at a time when they cannot so easily be exported North-South but are now threatening both of us together? (The North may be scrambling to deal with global warming, for example, but the South is still much more interested in bridging the gap in living standards.)

Further, pointing out the global nature of risk does not mean that we can assume that the risks are evenly spread. In general this sort of behaviour 'draws attention away from the necessity of emancipatory projects directed at the global underclasses' (10).

Finally, he also asks the question we have just asked ourselves: if it is true that the nation state is being undermined (or replaced by local government and civil society) have these developed sufficiently to provide the safety net once provided by the state?[15] We should at least be aware of what we are discarding.

For all these reasons and many more we live in an era of great insecurity and the natural reaction is that people are interested in security of the 'law and order' sort. They want to feel that they can sleep safely in their beds and indeed the Bible commends the institution of government in that it allows us to lead 'Godly and peaceable lives'.

There is a danger here, however. Security is also useful for 'business as usual'. It is in the interest of the 'haves' to be in control so that they can keep things quiet. Many business people see the state as primarily a mechanism within which they can make profits. For them, in the words of Joel Kovel, economic globalisation is little more than 'the establishment of a planetary scheme to supervise the expansionary process' (Kovel 2002, 68-9). Kovel suggests that capitalism is inherently 'global' and needs to dominate. 'It spreads faster, farther, draws more of the world into itself, restructuring production, circulation, exchange and consumption to accommodate its ever-growing pressure, in a logic that drives toward bringing the whole earth within the orbit of the dominant economic order.' (70). In order to do this it needs a trade organisation, a global bank and a financial enforcer and it already has these in the WTO, the World Bank and

15 Is this not the question that is being asked about David Cameron's 'Big Society'?

the IMF, which have either been created by, or bent to the will of, global capitalism. These institutions once served a wiser purpose and would have performed better had they retained it. When Keynes and his confederates introduced them after the Second World War they were not planning that they would become the vehicles of big business. The world at large knew only too well the disasters that capitalism could bring, which was why Keynes felt that some sort of regulation was needed, and why the Bretton Woods institutions were set up to provide it. But they have been subverted. Since the time of the Washington Consensus by and large they have become the instruments of a different purpose (Stiglitz 2002).

This process of global economic control can be seen in the different ways that different nations are treated by global institutions. The USA and Japan are the two great world debtors, but they have not been structurally adjusted! African countries by contrast, if they are to have their debts forgiven, must open up to the global economy, which includes controlling supposedly wasteful internal spending. As Kovel remarks:

> In other words: give us your forests and cheap labour by other means, and we will forgive the debt that you can't pay under any circumstances. (2002, 72)

The point of the illustration is that the system—we might simply call it capitalism—is dedicated to forgiving the rich and penalising the poor. Frankly, as Kovel warns, we must give up our idea that there are bad capitalists (say, the IMF) and good ones (the World Bank, perhaps). They are all one indivisible system. He illustrates this powerfully from the World Bank's dealings with Bolivia (73-4). For example, there is a continuum between governments, transnational corporations and mafias (74).

This sort of global economic control sounds uncomfortably like our old friend imperialism.[16] The trouble with imperialism, (Roman imperialism or British imperialism, for example) is not that it represents government as such, but that it is 'growth' government. It is committed as a first principle to its own aggrandisement. When people speak about the 'new imperialism' of the United States it is not because they are necessarily anti-American, but because they believe that its current policies are increasingly committed to putting its own interests above everybody else's. Even in the matter of the free market—something that it was assumed the US stood for—the US government was happy to protect its own steel industry when it felt that it was necessary to consult the needs of its own folk. So much for free trade! (Obviously even the Americans, with all their economic power, feel that they need their government to protect them from time to time.)

What sort of growth, if any, should we be interested in? Here is Simone Weil again:

16 I have written extensively on this topic in my recent book *Beyond Empire* (Ingleby 2010a).

> We accept material progress too easily as a
> gift of the gods, as something which goes
> without saying; we must look fairly and
> squarely at the conditions, at the cost of
> which, it takes place. (Weil 2001, 77)

Why do we so often use statistics to do with GDP
and economic ways of measuring as our final court of
appeal when we draw up the human balance sheet?
We know perfectly well that accountants only tell us
a very partial truth. Good work has been done in this
area by economists such as Amartya Sen who wants
us to talk about 'well-being' in a much more holistic
way (Sen 1999).

The Old Testament concept of *shalom* has this
broader view. It assumes that a man or a woman has
many enemies and to be truly prosperous needs to be
free from them all. Some are economic, some political, some reside in social structures, some are within.
The full life offers overarching security. We need a
safe place where good relationships can flourish and
the good life can be achieved. How much better a goal
like this than the reductive aim of raising people's
living standards.

A colleague of mine commented to me recently that
as far as his family was concerned their living standards had risen but their quality of life had fallen, and
that this was true for most of his neighbours as well.
He gave two interesting examples. His older children,
now grown up, had been much more free during their
childhood to leave the house and visit their friends
than his youngest child now was. She had the means
(a bicycle) but not the freedom. It was too dangerous,

much more dangerous than it used to be. The second example was of a neighbouring family who never had meals together. Life was very rushed, and in order to maintain their standard of living the family had to submit to living in that way. Admittedly, the fast food industry had made it easier to 'grab a meal on the run' but the question remained: had this produced a better quality of life than that enjoyed by societies who took time to eat at their leisure together?

These may seem trivial matters, but I doubt whether they are. Also, they are directly linked with globalisation. Families which are losing their sense of needing to be together and children who are increasingly at risk are symptoms of a much greater *malaise*. This *malaise* is linked to our pervasive global culture by many strands. To name but a few of them: greater social mobility—often necessary in order to find suitable work—making it difficult or impossible to maintain the extended family; supermarkets and fast-food outlets, making 'home cooking' comparatively expensive and time-consuming; entertainment industries that invade the home; societies increasingly dependent on the car, making our roads more dangerous for pedestrians and cyclists; adults who are so immersed in their jobs that they do not have time to entertain their friends at home; young people whose communication is reduced to the cell phone and the internet—better than nothing if you cannot go out to see your friends in the evening. Much of this destruction of the quality of life we once enjoyed has to do with the destruction of community. You only have to watch films like *La Gloire de mon Père* or *Le Châ-*

teau de ma Mère[17] with their celebration of family and family meals to realise how much we have lost. What is very disturbing is that there seems no way back, at least on a large scale. A younger generation do not even know what they are missing, and nobody in the complex world of globalisation is going to tell them. The Church could have a mission here and there are some aspects of modern church life, such as the *Alpha* courses, which suggest that there are still some possibilities of re-education.

Again, this may all seem rather trivial. We are not going to save the world by means of a few *Alpha* courses! But I am sure the issues to do with individuals and small communities are vitally linked with the ebb and flow of global affairs. Too much stress on economic 'growth' and insufficient emphasis on the quality of social life and the way it is developing is a macro and micro reality. Tom Sine warns us about 'the way in which the values of the marketplace seem increasingly to be shaping the values of human culture' (Sine 1999, 89). Martin Khor exhorts us to remember and emphasise the role of the United Nations. Why? 'Because of its indispensable and valuable role in advocating the social and developmental role in the process of global change.' He adds:

> The world, especially the developing countries, require that this dimension be kept alive and indeed strengthened greatly. (Khor 2001, 122)

---

17   The films were directed by Yves Robert and based on the famous novels of the same names by Marcel Pagnol.

Of course he is right, and it should set the whole tone of our planning for the future, but how difficult it is to make it a reality.

Another deity we encounter on the globalisation road is the great god Choice. In some ways this is an even more powerful force than the idea of Growth. The word is on the lips of every politician, spin doctor and salesperson that you meet. Why should people not have the possibility of choice, however? If young people have preferences that we disapprove of, well that is their preference! If Christians in other parts of the world wish to leap into modernity, surely that is up to them. Indeed if people in the West 'vote with their feet' as we say, in the direction of a globalised, free market, multi-choice world, then that is how it is. In any case, attempts to change this are like spitting in the wind.

It all sounds very plausible, but there are some questions that need answering. First of all, choice is often proffered in the name of freedom, and that has a good sound to it. Jesus said, however, that it is truth that makes us free. We need an effective value system if we are to be free to make the right choices in the first place. Also there is the related question of power. As Bob Dylan said 'You've got to serve somebody'. Who determines what choices I effectively have? Who controls the decision making process? Who says what I can do with my choices after I have made them? If I am unemployed and have no money in my pocket, being able to 'do whatever I like' does not feel much like choice. What are advertising and peer pressure and trendiness and good old fashioned ignorance do-ing to my ability to choose? Why do so many people choose things which are bad for them—like drugs, for example? And how real are the choices that I make in any case. I agonise over the right choice of after-shave lotion, pay a little bit extra for the brand name, and find that all the little bottles come from the same factory, though they have different labels on them.

No, it is not enough to offer 'more choice'. We need more 'truth', more education, more courage, more experience, more reality, if 'choice' is going to benefit us in the first place. Furthermore, what if multiplying my choices means diminishing the choices of others? The world's resources are after all limited, and competition for scarce resources very quickly becomes precisely the opposite of fair shares for all. We Christians, committed to big words like *koinonia*, fellowship, communion, sharing (all the same idea, of course) need to think carefully about this. Where there is a situation of winners and losers there is not a choice—people do not *choose* to be losers—more a question of ...winners and losers.

Let me attack another word beloved of the capital-ists—*competition*. As we know, the received wisdom in a capitalist society is that competition (winners and losers) is necessary, inevitable and indeed good. For one thing it drives down prices for us lucky consum-ers. It also increases choice (that word again) and stimulates growth. I wonder whether anybody has made an inventory of the dangers of competition. Let me attempt to do so.

It unfairly and unhealthily damages the producer, who has fixed costs which demand a return on his or her labour as a matter not of choice but of survival. In other words, consumers (I am including middle-men in this group) have far more choices than producers. At least this is true in a global market. The producer, I would contend, should have the *right* to receive a reasonable return, and this principle is a matter of mutual interest for both consumer and producer. So long as the consumer has the necessary means to live above the survival line it should be his or her aim, and indeed it is in his or her interest, to ensure that the producer does the same. At that basic level at least we should be in co-operation rather than competition. Globalisation makes this principle difficult to put into effect because we, the consumers, do not usually see the producers at work. Once upon a time when we lived together in villages, we could see very well if the main producers, the farmers, were failing and knew that it was in our interest that this should not happen. Today we know next to nothing about the conditions in which our food, or clothes, or household items are produced.

Competition leads to sharp practice, as night follows day. When you say something like this, you usually get two reactions. Firstly, that it is unfair to condemn a system by its faults. Of course there are the Enrons and Parmalats and plenty of little crooks as well. But you meet crooks in all walks of life, and it is unfair to single out business for special blame. The real culprit is not 'competition' but human nature.

But this is wrong. It is typical of the arguments that flow from an individualistic worldview. People are not autonomous agents. They act within a framework of beliefs and expectations. Their family socialises them into certain behaviour patterns. In time of

77

war their country expects them to go to war. Their business expects them to be competitive, to be 'ahead of the game', to take risks and to take the blame (ask Nick Leeson about this). There are powers in the land. Create a selfish society and people will act selfishly. Sit your youngsters in front of videos in which people are being slaughtered at regular intervals and before long you will have death in your schools. I was amused at the heading of a speech made by George W. Bush in response to the spate of corporate scandals that surfaced in the summer of 2002. It read 'In the long run there is no capitalism without conscience.' But there is, Mr President, there is.

The point is that we are encouraging our corporate leaders to lie. It is in their interest and the interest of their shareholders to 'talk up' their profits, for example. Any suggestion that profits are not what they ought to be—a 'profits warning'—and the confidence on which success is built in the business world is eroded. It is not a coincidence that businesses pretend that they are doing well when they are not, it is part of the game. Illusions which can be maintained long enough turn into realities. Fostering the illusions is, frankly good business. (A bank manager friend of mine was told by his superiors that he could not buy a Vauxhall; bank managers drove BMWs or the equivalent; the confidence of the customers in the bank and its prosperity as represented by the manager's car, needed to be maintained at all costs—even if, presumably, the bank had fallen on hard times and would have benefited by providing cheaper company cars to its managers.)

It is often suggested that competition is a 'law of nature', in the sense that it is folly to suggest that we can base our behaviour on any other system. Other systems simply do not work. Children, we are told, are inherently competitive, and this is healthy. Even if it is not healthy, it is certainly the case.

One of the reasons why I am not convinced by this argument is that, in my experience, it is possible to maintain high standards without drawing on a competitive ethos. Two of the Christian organisations for which I have worked have managed to do this. It may be that this is partly because they are Christian, but this does not negate the point. The people working in these organisations were, and are, ordinary human beings. Yet something happened to change what was supposedly the norm of competitiveness and, I would maintain, the outcome was to produce something better.

In one case at least, what was taken out of the system was financial gain. The organisation—it was a school—worked on the basis that all were paid the same wage, from the most senior to the most junior, from the newest recruit to the oldest of old hands, from the highly qualified to the relatively uneducated. The only variation of salary depended on the size of the family. People, in other words, were equally rewarded for their work. Everybody was expected to work, but the nature of the work load was determined individually, allowing for different work capacities and other non-school responsibilities. There was a hierarchy, based in the usual way on ability to do the job, but no perks attached to it. Meals were taken in common, transport was shared, friends and family were welcome to stay without charge. Food, accommodation, heating and medical care, were all provided. The only major personal expenses were leisure activities, including holidays, and clothes. The community met together once a week for prayer and discussion, and decisions which affected the community were taken together at that time. Everybody had a voice. Notice that this was a school. It entered the students for the usual examinations—GCSE and A Levels—and results had to satisfy the parents, otherwise, as the headmaster used to say, no matter how much they liked the ethos of the school they would take their children away. However, results were good, indeed the students did exceptionally well. This was partly because of the school's atmosphere and the co-operation of the parents, but also because, perhaps surprisingly, the school never had any difficulty in recruiting gifted, conscientious and reliable staff. In a number of cases it was highly instructive to watch new staff members who had come out of much more 'competitive' staff rooms, learning with some difficulty that 'the angel' of the school (its ethos, or style, or tradition, or spirituality) had a different face. It was, so to speak, a non-competitive face.

This description may sound impossibly idealised. Was everything 'sweetness and light'? Of course not, and that is not what I am saying. What I am saying is that the system was different. There were plenty of painful moments, failures as well as successes. But overall the thing worked. I am encouraged to make such a claim because I have encountered this phenomenon more than once. After leaving the school I have described I worked in two educational organisations whose 'angels' were grotesquely disfigured, the one by the spirit of greed and the other by violence and despair. Since then, thankfully, I have been able to experience again a space where justice, peace, mercy and truth (Psalm 85:10) have made a life of genuine sharing possible. In this space too, the supposedly indispensable characteristic of competitiveness has been absent, and yet really excellent work goes on all the time.

Just in case we might think that these examples are little more than tiny exceptions to the uncomfortable reality of society as it actually performs, we can remind ourselves that our 'dog eats dog' world has always had its critics. Some of the great political and economic thinkers of the past were quite prepared to challenge 'economism' (that economics are everybody's 'bottom line') and propose alternatives. David Smith writes:

> [John] Ruskin is an example of somebody who clearly pointed out the disaster into which economism was leading industrial society and who was at the same time stumbled by the unwillingness of supposedly practising Christians to confront this issue.
> (Smith D. 2003, 90-91)

When Ruskin wrote the first of his three essays which now make up 'Unto This Last' (1860) the most controversial issue he introduced was the idea of a citizen's wage (Ruskin 1862, 107-8). It was an idea—'the organisation of labour with fixed wages' he called it—which he defended with his usual passion and brilliance and which, in my opinion, enshrines a 'kingdom principle'. When Jesus told the story of the workers in the vineyard who were hired at different intervals during the day, but who all got the same wage (Matthew 20:1-16 and parallels) we customarily take this to be an illustration of the grace of God. God gives freely to us all that we need, whether we deserve it or not. But perhaps the story is just as much about the economic principles applied to the labour market where labour is at a disadvantage. Then its main point would be that it is 'fair' that people should be paid 'according to their need', rather than according to what they have contributed. As commentators have pointed out, the wage paid was not a generous one, (Herzog 1994, 89) it was a 'living wage' in the strict sense. Without it, and without any other means of support, people would perish. This is not a story about laziness or fear of risk (that is another parable). People wanted to work, but there was no work to be had.

If we imagine that many of the people who were listening to this story had been in precisely this situation, then the interpretation I have suggested begins to take on a good deal of interest for them. The 'grace of God' as explained above, may seem a somewhat abstract theory, particularly if you and your family are starving. A 'kingdom' in which there is provision for all, even if there is not enough work to go round, would be a very exciting prospect.

Ruskin's title 'Unto This Last' reminds me of something else. It was to 'the last' that the owner gave most generously, in the sense that he received proportionately the highest rate of pay. In Matthew

20:16, Jesus' conclusion to the story is that the last will be first and the first last. But that is not the only time that he uses these words. The 'upside down kingdom' is a familiar theme in Jesus' teaching. (See e.g. Matthew 19:30 where the context is also one of economic arrangements.)

What are the barriers to this idea that we should have a citizen's wage—I mean barriers in *our* society? At a very fundamental level it is not part of our 'plausibility structure'. We do not think it could work, however good the idea might be in principle. The fact that the interpretation of the parable that I have suggested has not often been suggested (I have never come across it in a sermon, for example) may be for this very reason—it does not look like practical politics, so let's look around for some 'spiritual' interpretation. Then again we are not all that happy about Jesus' 'upside down kingdom'. As far as we are concerned that first will be first and the last last and a jolly good thing too! It affronts our *moral* sense that we 'haves' are somehow not quite so deserving as we thought we were, and worse still, we are to be rewarded to the same extent as those 'have-nots', wastrels and layabouts who stood around all day when we were working hard.

We are also very frightened of the idea of a citizen's wage because we think that there will be a vast number of people who will immediately become loafers and spongers, happily drawing their weekly pay cheque and doing nothing to deserve it. (Even Ruskin could not tolerate this thought. See Ruskin 1862, 127.) This is nonsense. Give people adequate incentives and they will work. I lived for several years on a housing estate in this country where there was considerable unemployment and many of the people were on benefits. Did they sit around doing nothing? Not at all. Admittedly many of them had found work through what is euphemistically called the 'informal economy' but that does not disprove my point. I also worked for many years in India. The record of the British Raj is littered with complaints that Indians are naturally lazy. And yet migrant Indians and independent Indians working for themselves will soon be ruling the world!

The other argument you hear is that we cannot afford a citizen's wage. That is probably true unless we are prepared to accept an equalisation of wealth. Perhaps the worker (in the parable) who complained would have been happy enough for the others to receive a day's wage so long as he was paid *extra* for working longer than they did. But perhaps the owner could not afford to pay extra. He could only afford to pay higher wages than the going rate if he paid lower wages (i.e. lower than a day's pay) to those who had come late on the job. A famous British Chancellor of the Exchequer once said that 'we shall have to tax the rich to help the poor'.[18] Not so different an idea perhaps. The point is that good economic arrangements begin with a sufficiency for all. Only after you have settled that matter should you think about bonuses. (I am not saying that you can get that out of the parable, only that that is kingdom economics.)

The matter of incentives is a complicated one. The mistake is to think that money is the *only* effective

18 The key theme of David Lloyd George's 'People's Budget' in 1909.

incentive. John Ruskin nailed this argument in the same essay to which we have been referring. What he calls 'the social affections' are all those other factors apart from the accumulation of wealth that, he says, should contribute to our thinking about the science of political economy. If these are neglected the best results cannot be obtained.

> The largest quantity of work...will be done only when the motive force, that is to say, the will or spirit of the creature, is brought to the greatest strength by its own proper fuel; namely by the affections. (121)

In more modern language, the best results will be obtained when people love and enjoy their work, trust the people they are working for and with, and use their gifts in a fulfilling way.

My own experiences, described above, and the encouragement of thinkers like Ruskin, have made me a (Christian) communist. 'From each according to his or her ability, to each according to his or her need' seems to me eminently fair, doable and Christian. I am not convinced that competitiveness makes for efficiency. I am not even in favour of competing against myself. Grace is better than law, and 'driven' people are not really healthy and effective. Power corrupts and becomes an end in itself.

> For Marx showed clearly that the true reason for the exploitation of the workers is not any desire on the part of the capitalists to enjoy and consume, but the need to expand

> the undertaking as rapidly as possible so
> as to make it more powerful than its rivals.
> (Weil 2001, 39)

By taking my examples from education it may be felt that I have chosen a soft target. (But you will not find many teachers who agree with you!) Does this also apply to the world of business and politics? I think it does. Business people often claim that theirs is a harsh world and that people enter it for the rewards which only really fall to those who get to the top. Another way of putting this is that incentives are essential to business enterprise. Even if you knock out the idea of competition (i.e. a sort of survival of the fittest) you have to give people something to aim at: promotion, higher wages, better quality of life. Communism does not work precisely because these incentives are effectively removed. Having contributed what I can, and received what I need, then there is no new place to go to.

My reply is that incentives are only good when they are for a good purpose, and that we need to put the emphasis on incentives of love rather than incentives of greed or aggrandisement. Of course people need good reasons for doing things. Of course, this need extends to business life. People simply will not perform for no good reason. So we need to look around for these incentives of love: love for God, love for my neighbour, love for my students, love for my patients, love for my business partners, even love for my boss or love for my customers. Christians are expected to go further and love their rivals and enemies but I am trying to describe something here which can be recommended as a working ethic for the whole of society.

To ask the question again: do we accept competition as the only basis of business motivation? Do we have to? An interesting insight into this is given by writers on management theory. They are at pains to emphasise that businesses should be concerned not with selling but with marketing. The point is that business needs to define its goal as the satisfaction of the customer's needs. So the key question is not 'What do we want to sell?' but 'What does the customer want to buy?'

Now this is a sort of love. It is an attitude that looks to the needs of others. I am not talking here about the personal motivation of the businessman, but rather about the attitude which the customer perceives as informing the firm's business transactions. It is a 'loving' attitude based on the consumer's needs, and it is good business. Thus there are firms that we trust such as Sony or BMW (whether we are right to do so or not) which make money at a tremendous rate, because they have a reputation for giving their customers a square deal and looking after them.

As part of my attempt to apply these ideas to local situations where Christians can be involved, I would like to cite the example of a relative of mine. For many years he ran a chemist's shop in Parkstone in Dorset. It was not a big business but it was a thriving one. Perhaps the main reason for this was that everybody in the neighbourhood knew 'Foster's the Chemist' as a shop where Mr Foster knew you! He remembered people's names, spoke to people as if they mattered, shared their concerns and their aspirations, enquired after sick relatives, offered well-considered advice, never seemed to be in a hurry. No doubt you get the picture.

The point is that it was good for *business*. Knowing Mr Foster I am sure that that is not *why* he behaved as he did. But whatever the motive it certainly worked.

Again, there are plenty of people who would say that this is hopelessly unrealistic. I am not convinced. I suspect that many, even among those who make that sort of remark, have a secret hankering for the days when idealism ('love' if you like) was a more valued part of our society, when, for example, people were happy to claim that they had a sense of vocation or that they worked for a 'good' firm. We are very cynical about these ideas today, perhaps because people's idealism has been all too often exploited, used as a reason for underpaying them, for example. Certainly, as we have said, we need caring employers as well as faithful employees. But as so often, we are apt to condemn something good, because it has been abused. Love can be abused but it does not make it any the less essential.

Big firms can be loved and trusted but it is easier to do good relationships on a smaller scale. That is another reason why economic globalisation is often a second best. Multinationals tend to offer (they have no choice about this) customer relations (usually at the end of some infuriating process of dialling the right numbers—'if you want customer relations press 1'—and a spell listening to piped music—'all our lines are busy at the moment') rather than personal relations (Mr Foster). The fact that I can dial up customer relations from my home or my mobile, whereas to speak to Mr Foster I have to venture forth into the High Street is not, to me, much of a consolation. What we call better communications, a supposed feature of globalisation, is often nothing of the sort. Suffice it to say that I agree with Richard Rogers (Reith Lectures 1995) that we should denounce the idea that 'modern life is about staying in the security of our own homes, about shopping, working and interacting across an electronic network, without any physical contact'. Instead, 'face-to-face contact, the chance encounter, proximity, these have been essential components of humanity'. Exactly.

Face-to face contact takes time, and we are always trying to save time, but this compulsion may also be part of the capitalist trap. As Joel Kovel has pointed out, in the capitalist order the value of commodities is only realised as they are exchanged, that is to say circulated and exchanged for money. For capital to 'grow' its realisation must speed up; its circulation time must be diminished. But the way time is viewed by capitalism is part of its rupture from nature. Capitalism becomes obsessed with time and it is a different time scale from that of most ecosystems. This relentless speeding-up has numerous consequences. It leads to the managerial society. Human relations have to be engineered, with all the dishonesties that that produces. It leads to waste, the throw-away society. It leads to the fear of growing old and out-dated. The boundary marks between work and home disappear, as do those between the body and the machine. 'More and more, people scramble, becoming increasingly obsessed with money, and slaves to the system' (Kovel 2002, 62-3). It takes over everything. An advert for American Express reads 'We're here to help you do *more*' (Kovel 2002, 63-4). But is that a threat or a promise?

Let me go back to the idea of freedom. As we have seen, words like 'choice', 'enterprise', 'opportunity' even 'competition' are often linked with the word 'free'. 'Freedom' in fact is a word which has largely been appropriated by 'free-market' capitalism. So we are in favour of 'free societies' and these only work if we have 'free trade'. (I heard somebody say this in a debate on capitalism just the other day.) Words like 'regulation' (worse still 'rules' which means the same thing) 'controls', 'intervention', 'barriers' (as in tariff) seem by contrast unfree.

A friend of mine once remarked that he would rather see advertising (however blatant and dishonest) on the hoardings than political slogans. I can see his point, but nevertheless I do not feel that we can take this argument too far. Surely we all agree that some government regulation is necessary. Simply maintaining law and order is a form of government intervention. Nor can you divorce the economic sphere of life from other spheres. Censorship of pornographic materials is, among other things, a form of economic control. We do not think that people should be allowed to exploit children and teenagers in the name of a 'free' economy. In fact I think that direct economic regulation, such as health and safety regulations or even minimum wages, is approved of by most people, certainly by most Christians, however capitalist. After all we know that child labour in the coal mine and sixteen hours a day in the factory were once common enough in Britain, and that they have not entirely disappeared from our world today either. Even in the United States, one of the world's wealthiest countries, working all hours of the day, seven days a week, still may not make it possible to pay the rent and the grocer's bill if you get stuck in a 'minimum wage' job such as waitressing, cleaning, store assistant and the like (Ehrenreich 2002).

The question is not government regulation but how much and what sort. I heard Vandana Shiva say once that the agenda of the wealthy and powerful nations represented by the G8 was not deregulation but reregulation. Not doing away with rules but drawing them up anew in a way that worked best for them.

> The global marketplace, left to itself, is not going to automatically produce wealth and prosperity in less-developed countries unless there is rule-making and new structures that reduce the potential for destructiveness.
> (Schaeffer 2003, 245)

The question, in other words, is not about whether we regulate or not, but 'whose rules rule', as the World Development Movement slogan puts it.

Are there arguments in favour of the present mode of economic globalisation? There are indeed, though unsurprisingly they mostly come from the spokespeople of the business world, such as *The Economist* magazine and popular 'Western' voices such as TIME magazine. I do think, however, that since the 2008 banking crisis, the *moral* high ground seems to have been grabbed by the anti-globalisers, who are making their point more effectively, or at least more brazenly, that their opponents. There is something surprising about this particularly when we consider that the protesters are, by most standards, a rather unprepossessing bunch and have powerful governments, big business, and most of the media (who are owned by big business) ranged against them. Consider, also, that the protesters have nothing much to gain by their activities. Not many of them will get an invitation to the Waldorf-Astoria to attend an international business forum. Rather, they cancel their holidays, camp out in all weathers, risk getting beaten by overzealous policeman, and try once again to claim the attention of those who are systematically backing their own greedy and aggressive lifestyle against the poor and downtrodden of the earth. So why do they do it? Perhaps they know that they are in the right; they have justice on their side, and are prepared to make sacrifices because of it.

At the risk of being repetitive let me suggest that the case in favour of economic globalisation falters at two crucial points.

Firstly, despite all the rhetoric, we have failed to translate free trade into fair trade. Anti-globalisers are not against trade, they are against the way that trade is set up so that some benefit at the expense of others. The whole concept of growth is far too vague. The fact that the world economy is growing, or that a country's economy is growing, is only a part of the picture. The truth is that we ought to measure 'growth' and prosperity, in the first instance, from the vantage point of the poor. This is a very difficult thing to do. Governments and NGOs almost always end up in a situation where they need to ally themselves with the rich and powerful (landowners or people with education or opinion formers) in order to get things done. Usually they are happy enough with this situation, if only because they themselves come from the same background and share the same aspirations. As long as 'our kind of folk' are prospering, then that is progress. It is not that these people are necessarily hypocritical and selfish. They just cannot see what they need to see in order to assess the situation accurately.

(Preachers of the Gospel as well as those bringing humanitarian aid encounter the same difficulty. When Jesus said that he was proclaiming 'good news to the poor' he did not mean that he wished to exclude the rich from hearing the Gospel. He was saying that the rich *found it very difficult* to understand and accept the Gospel. This would continue until they gave up their riches, and then of course they would see things from the point of view of the poor.)

On a recent trip to India I kept my eyes open and asked everybody I could whether things were 'better'. Almost everybody I asked said that they were. But the important question I never really had answered was: better for whom? The people I talked to were English speakers (otherwise I could not have conversed with them) who travelled air-conditioned as I did, who, like me, used reasonably priced hotels (not five star of course, but still well out of the reach of the majority of Indians) who had a good education and who certainly did not spend each day worrying where the next meal would come from. But what would it have been like if I had talked to the slum dwellers in Kolkata, or the peasant sharecroppers in some remote village in Bihar? I will never really know the answer to that question, but my guess is that they would not have said that 'things were better'.

Just to back up my personal impressions I add those of the Canadian journalist, John Stackhouse. Stackhouse was based in New Delhi from 1992-1999 and has written a remarkable account of what he saw and did (Stackhouse 2000). The key to his journalism, it seems to me, is that he quite deliberately chose to spend most of his time with the poor. In New Delhi he witnessed the considerable wealth that the liberalisation of the economy brought to the nation, or at least to some in the nation. Yet he visited again and again a little village called Biharipur in Madhya Pradesh, some 300 kilometres from Delhi, in order to chronicle *its* progress, if that is the word. It is not the word. The villagers were slipping backward. Anybody who has read Jeremy Seabrook's *In the Cities of the South* (Seabrook 1996) will know that what really matters in doing urban sociology is the 'feel' of actually lived experience among the 'wretched of the earth'.

Secondly, who pays for growth? Are the earth's resources unlimited? They certainly are not, but the trouble with globalisation is that it knows no limits. As Terry Eagleton has remarked:

> Radical politics... is an exceedingly modest proposal. Bertolt Brecht once remarked that it was capitalism, not communism, which was radical, and his colleague Walter

> Benjamin added wisely that revolution was
> not a runaway train but the application of
> the emergency brake. It is capitalism which
> is out of control, and socialism which seeks
> to restrain it... It is a sign of just how bad
> things are that even the modest proposal
> that everyone on the planet should get fresh
> water and enough to eat is fighting talk.
> (*New Statesman* January 2002, 19)

Also, are there never any occasions when there is *harmful* competition for resources (and the scarcer they get the more ruthless the competition will be)? Let me give a simple example. The tourist trade has brought wealth and 'development' to Goa on the west coast of India—economic growth, at least by one definition. However, there is a downside. Hotels which aspire to 'Western' standards need a great deal of water, particularly in a hot climate. This they have the power to commandeer in the name of 'growth' and 'development'. And who loses out? The villagers living just beyond the shore line who once had wells which provided them with water for drinking, cooking and agriculture, discover that their wells are drying up. You can multiply this picture a million times. The trouble with globalisation is that it is based on this sort of competition. It does not know how to thrive except at the expense of others less fortunate, or weaker, or less ruthless.

Finally, and by way of summary, I would like to take up some ideas that Anthony Giddens has stressed in his book *Runaway World* (1999). Giddens points out that globalisation is not just what is happening in the

market place. It is a widespread and varied phenomenon. By its very nature it undermines and overrides
the appeal to local custom and practice. He gives some
examples, and I add some reflections from a Christian
and missiological perspective.

New patterns of sexuality, marriage and family whereby women are staking a claim to greater
autonomy and entering the labour force in larger
numbers, is a form of globalisation. How do women
now respond to a church if it refuses to support them
in their new and demanding roles?

In a world where information and images are
shared world-wide, cultural complexity is here to
stay. Of course, many find it disturbing, and the result
is a growing fundamentalism.

> Whether in the areas of religion, ethnic identity
> or nationalism, they take refuge in a renewed
> and purified tradition. (Giddens 1999, 6)

Is Christianity also 'fundamentalist' in character?
Are we inclined to fight one fundamentalism with
another? Is this not a tiger from which we may find it
difficult to dismount?

With the end of the cold war ('the end of history')
the orthodoxy is that there is only one economic system. The era of the global media, for example, fatally
undermined the Soviet system after 1970. Now there
are no Berlin walls and iron curtains, and almost
every boundary is porous. The remotest regions are
reached by satellite technology. Are there not huge
opportunities for the church in a situation where eth-

nic and national boundaries can no longer keep out information from elsewhere?

Globalisation squeezes sideways, creating new economic and cultural zones, for example Hong Kong, North Italy or Barcelona and its region. What sort of challenge do the new economic regions pose to the accuracy of our missiological maps, which perhaps are drawn up overmuch on the basis of ethnicity?

Globalisation itself is becoming increasingly de-centred, i.e. not under anyone's control. For example, 'reverse-colonisation' is here to stay, despite the best efforts of the West to resist the process through immigration laws, discrimination and the like. Los Angeles has been latinised, Indian restaurants are the most frequented in the UK, and Brazilian cultural products such as music and films have largely taken over the Portuguese market. If 'reverse-colonisation' is already an economic reality need 'reverse-mission' be far behind?

Postmodernism

It is easier I think to define postmodernism in terms of what it is not than to say what it is. Even its most famous definition, Lyotard's 'a suspicion of metanarratives', tends to take this approach. This may help us. Christians are often as suspicious of the follies of modernity as anybody else. We realise that some of the ideologies which have made a claim to be universal have done a huge amount of damage, particularly in the century just past. Perhaps it is even true to say that attempts to mould the social world have generally led to tyranny. We also feel, or should feel, that there is something ugly about the way that people claim that *their* truth relativises everybody else's. For example, Christian evangelists and missionaries have not always in the past been sufficiently careful about the dangers of empire building based on their own interpretation of cultural norms.

Whether we sympathise or not with the discourse of postmodernism it is certain that it would be foolish to ignore it. There is a tendency among Christians, particularly of a certain generation, to treat postmodernism as an intellectual fashion or fad, something which, if we are patient, will go away. I think this is a mistake. I would say that postmodernism is an outcome of several trends—late capitalism, including greater customer choice, a more risky world, multiculturalism and the advance of the Global South—some of which we have already noted as features of globalisation, and none of which are likely to go away. Young people in the West now largely grow up in a postmodern society and have never known anything else. Postmodernism has become 'the atmosphere we breathe' and when the church attempts to distance itself from it, it can only do so by creating a sort of bubble in which church people can breathe but others find the atmosphere too rarefied. I am not saying, of course, that we have to go along with everything postmodernism stands for, but rather that we cannot realistically ignore it, wishing that the world were different than it in fact is.

The problem with modernity is that it lacks humility. It is a project that is based on certainties that are not quite so certain as we like to think. Human reason is not the instrument we once believed it to be—all sorts of thinkers and ideas in recent times have dethroned rationality from its position of unquestioned authority. As a result, science is also not the enterprise we thought it to be, not in fact the surefooted guide we felt we could trust implicitly. The idea of progress itself—the feeling that we shall get there in the end, wherever 'there' is, as long as we keep going—seems only one possibility. There are plenty of people nowadays predicting the possibility of regress, even decline and fall. Can we design the ideal society, the beautiful city, the earthly paradise, or have the hopes we placed in social engineering finally been dashed? These are some of the doubts and questions that fill our minds when we think about modernity.

Has the modern project really come to a halt? What about the growth of technological innovation, perhaps especially the information and communications revolutions? What about the advances in medical science? Also, if progress is a little difficult to be sure of, what about growth? More and more people are buying into the technology revolution, for example. Whatever our fears for the future, surely it is a blessing that more people have more choice. The Chinese peasant may face harsh conditions in the cutthroat booming commercial cities of Eastern China, but at least he or she is not trapped in the no-choice existence of subsistence agriculture.

The ideas of greatly expanded growth and choice should remind us of postmodernism's relation to capitalism, as in Frederic Jameson's famous essay: *Postmodernism, or the Cultural Logic of Late Capitalism* (Jameson 1992). Capitalism 'old-style', often called

'Fordism', was characterised by mass production of standardised products, assembly lines, the division of labour, reliability and long-life as standard, and relatively low prices. It was not particularly interested in consumer *choice*. 'Any colour, so long as it's black' as Henry Ford is supposed to have said about choice of car colour, as the Model T Ford rolled off the production line. Now consumer choice demands something else, and this is by no means an insignificant change. It signals that late capitalism is driven by the desire for novelty and innovation, for style rather than substance, for an acceptance of ephemerality and obsolescence, for 'a culture of shopping' (or just browsing and window-shopping) for brands and logos and fashions. This cultural and economic 'turn' makes it difficult for there to be any real engagement with history, or indeed with settled certainties. My point here is that postmodernism is the product of cultural and economic forces that are a familiar part of our world—'shopping rules OK' for example—not just some academic theory. As I say, we have no choice but to come to terms with it.

Certainties are breaking down at another level. All those metanarratives that the twentieth century relied upon to 'build a new world'—liberal democracy, socialism, national self-determination, have become tarnished, even thought to be obsolete. In its own sceptical way postmodernism has led us out into the wilderness where the familiar signposts have disappeared and has left us there. So the question is not 'where am I?', or 'where do I go next?, but 'can I survive'?. Besides which, in the wilderness all too often I find that I am fending for myself. There used to be a common cause and a common destination, but the familiar communities are no longer there to support us. If I am going to survive I am going to have to defend myself against possible dangers. The desert is a lonely pace but that does not mean that there are no enemies.

You may say that I am speaking too much in parables. Let me give you a couple of concrete examples. The family used to provide people with their social security (and still does in many parts of the world). Among other types of provision, the elderly were cared for by the extended family. To some extent in the wealthy industrialised nations, the state took over the duty of caring for the elderly. This was partly because the structure of industrialised society was different, but it was also part of the socialist idea, particularly the provision of Old Age Pensions. Now it may be that this too is breaking down in an increasingly individualised society. People not only have less support from the family, but state socialism is in decline. What then? One result is that old age is more risky. A safety-net has been withdrawn. Take a look at what has happened to many old people in the former Soviet Union.

Another example: jobs used to be for life. You entered the firm as a young person, were trained on the job, moved steadily through the ranks up to your level of ability, became a trusted member of the organisation, and finally retired with an occupational pension. Unless you were unlucky, there was no reason why the system should not sustain you and your family for life. Today, however, in our postmodern, post-Fordist world the risks are of a completely different order. I do not need to spell them out in detail, but it is certain that job security is a thing of the past.

It was much easier to cling on to cultural certainties when we lived in relatively homogeneous societies. There were always people who were different from us, of course, but we lived in nations where these different people were either visitors who would soon go away, or strangers who were expected to abandon their own cultures and conform to ours. When we travelled abroad, even if we intended to remain there, 'home' was always where we derived from. Intermarriage between those of different cultures was considered to be very much the exception—even wrong—and certainly very difficult. People from the Global South were often despised.

Sadly, these attitudes are still with us, but given that nowadays we consistently meet people from the South who are cleverer, more successful and better educated than we are, it is difficult to go on with the fiction of superiority. Besides, much of what we encounter from other cultures (think Indian restaurants) is thoroughly enjoyable. There is a good deal of exchange. The West has had to learn that people different from ourselves can do things better than we can (think Japanese electronics) and we are happy to buy into their success. These familiar developments create a much less certain sense of cultural identity, contributing, as we have said, to the eroding of the certainties which previously undergirded Western modernity.

There is a full-scale debate to be had here about what a church in a postmodern society should look like. It is, in fact, the old contextualisation debate. If the wealthy nations of the West are increasingly postmodern in outlook, church planters and builders must take that into account. People coming from a non-Western culture, especially people who have themselves been brought up in an exported Western modernity, may find this very confusing.

Postcolonialism

Postcolonialism is a term which aims to express the huge change which has come about in our world as a result of the disintegration of the great European empires over the last fifty or sixty years. In examining this process it wants us to note that:

- There was resistance to colonialism even when colonialism was at its highest point.

- The history of the colonised nations has been written by the colonists.

- The colonial presence repressed and 'buried' many aspects of the life of the colonised nation: these elements may perhaps still be recovered.

- Since independence certain aspects of colonialism have been transmitted to the 'inheritors' who have sometimes themselves become a colonial elite.

- Colonialism of the traditional variety, involving the occupation of territory and the blatant exploitation of resources, has given way in an uncomfortably large number of cases, to neo-colonialism, by which the Western powers continue to exploit former colonies (and others) by economic means (occasionally backed up by superior firepower!).

Colonialism continues to have long-drawn-out political, economic, cultural and especially demographic global consequences. Take for example the widespread migration of previously colonised peoples to the countries which originally colonised them (e.g. North Africans to France, West Indians to the UK, Indonesians to Holland); another example would be the widespread continued use of the European languages worldwide.

The postcolonial world is now so thoroughly mixed that the future is not simply multicultural but hybrid.

I have tried to spell out in my book *Beyond Empire* (Ingleby 2010a) some of the consequences of postcolonialism for mission. There I use the word in two senses: that we are living in an era after the fall of the great (largely) European empires and that postcolonialism refers to a new way of looking at the world i.e. through a postcolonial lens. Here I simply want to say that postcolonialism is our context, which like postmodernism and globalisation cannot be ignored. If you do not believe me, just try standing for a while in one of the busy (are there any other sort?) terminals at Heathrow Airport and see what you make of it!

Migration/Movement

All commentators agree that people are on the move as never before, and will continue to be so. The global culture demands and then favours those who are prepared to be mobile or at least to plug into the communications revolution at some level. This does not mean of course that all of the people washing around our world are where they are by choice.

'Economic migrants' is a loaded term, nowadays, but we should remember that they come in a number of varieties. They may be people who simply want to earn a better living, and have marketable skills for which they can get a better price away from home. (Oddly enough, considering the outrage commonly expressed in affluent countries about 'economic migrants', *some* of these people appear to be welcome outside their own countries. Britain, for example, recruits staff for the National Health Service from all over the world at the moment. This just goes to show that our response to migrants is largely selfish. If we judge them necessary to meet our needs, we are happy to have them; if not, not.)

Then there are those who need to make new arrangements for their families as a matter of survival. They simply cannot provide for their own by staying at home. Globalisation in its revolutionary communications mode has made these movements possible where they have not always been an option before. Relatively cheap international transport—say, from India to the Arab Gulf states—has meant hundreds of thousands of impoverished Indians earning their living in the Middle East.

Also, sometimes globalisation is the cause of this process. The way in which multi-nationals can now choose where their manufacturing and service base is, means that for many people the work which was traditionally associated with their locality has gone elsewhere and they simply have to travel away from home in order to move to a new job. Then there are the refugees from war and from religious and political persecution. In some ways most people in the affluent world are economic migrants. Very few people stay at home when it comes to finding a job. The difference is that globalisation has made it both easier and (sometimes) more necessary to make that move. Not equally easy, however. Unequal development within globalisation means job mobility and open frontiers for some, it means forced migration and hostile frontiers for others.

Many of these people on the move find themselves in our cities. Global cities are another feature of economic globalisation. This does not simply mean that there are more and bigger cities. This is certainly true, and poorer migrants will be found in their slums and ghettos, along with refugees from the local countryside. It is also true, however, that cities are being re-created by globalisation. They begin to take on a role which gives them global connections such as an international airport, electronic communication systems, prestigious banks, and good leisure and entertainment facilities for guests, including good hotels. For many people it then becomes important to move to, or continue to live in, the city because, for the 'haves' it gives these better connections with the globe, and for the rest it gives access to the jobs that service them. Many of the former are members of what has been called 'the epistemic community', comprised of people who make their living because they have specialist knowledge and can contribute it to society in a useful way.

Once upon a time, wealth was measured largely by possession of land, and all sorts of power flowed from being a landowner. Particularly if you were a really big landowner then the gifted—craftsmen, musicians, poets, architects, merchants—earned their livings through your patronage. Now the knowledge experts—especially in finance or communications, but also in advertising or management, have power of their own. A society and a culture, so dependent on money flows and sophisticated communications, on skilful management and image presentation, has found work for these gifted people to do. Further, epistemic communities tend to flourish in a high risk world. Because we feel we cannot control our lives and because the future seems so uncertain we turn to the experts. Which of us does not hope that our financial adviser—if we have one!—is a little further ahead of the game than we are when it comes to planning our pensions.

We have already mentioned the increasing economic insecurity, particularly in terms of safe jobs. This is an important part of the picture when we try to discern the reasons for increased global mobility. There are few jobs for life and having to move to keep your job or to acquire re-training is common. Far from condemning people for being 'economic migrants' we should congratulate those who willing to take this responsibility for determining their own life paths, while remembering that this may be a hugely stressful process. Zygmunt Bauman describes it like this:

> With skills falling out of demand in less time
> than it takes to acquire and master them,
> with educational credentials losing value
> against their cost of purchase by the year
> or even turning into 'negative equity' long
> before their allegedly lifelong 'sell-by' date,
> with places of work disappearing with little
> or no warning, and with the course of life
> sliced into a series of ever shorter one-off
> projects, life prospects look increasingly
> like the haphazard convolutions of smart
> rockets in search of elusive, ephemeral and
> restless targets, rather than a predesigned
> and predetermined, predictable trajectory of
> a ballistic missile. (Bauman 2003, 91)

This insecurity is the down-side of a world in which choice is now available on a global scale. Businesses that are big enough and clever enough to be attuned to global trends can use their global vision to their advantage. They can work out what are the local 'bargains', where the cheapest labour is situated, which locality has which skills at the best price, who wants to buy what where, and put all this information to good use. But what are the personal costs? People in localities are well aware that this sort of reconnaissance, and desperately do their best to shape up to expectations, in the hope of attracting what is called 'foreign direct investment'.

Even this can be counterproductive. Local people abandon their distinctives if they think that would be more attractive to global investors, only to find, ironically, that in the long term this destroys the distinctiveness which was the very reason for which they were selected in the first place!

Place

My thinking in this whole area has flowed largely from Raymond Williams, particularly his novels. Williams, a socialist and a sociologist, was very interested in the idea of cultural holism. He thought that social practices were 'indissoluble elements of a continuous material process' (Harvey 1996, 24) and that human beings are only able to maintain common values by means of 'a certain kind of interpersonal relating that typically occurs in particular places' (29). Williams' last and unfinished novel *People of the Black Mountains* (1990 & 1992) begins in 23,000 BCE and traces the social and environmental history of the Black Mountains from that date onwards, calling in at high and low points in the locality's history—the great ice age, the advent of settled agriculture, the coming of literacy and so on. This seems an odd approach for a social scientist perhaps, but Williams insisted that social beings can never escape this embeddedness in the world of nature.

> Once we begin to speak of mixing their labour with the earth, we are in a whole world of new relations between men and nature and to separate natural history from social history becomes extremely problematical.
> (Harvey 1996, 26)

Or, to put it more simply, there is a process going on by means of which we shape our environment and our environment shapes us. Thus place = history + nature. Of course, history includes all the outside influences that a place is subject to—dramatic ones like invasions, or more subtle ones like the arrival of a missionary or the influence of traders.

Williams was also interested in describing a number of tensions which he believed existed between the local and the cosmopolitan. He was the son of a Welsh railwayman and brought up in a small Welsh village, but he won a place at Cambridge and became an academic. The protagonist in his first novel *Border Country* (Williams 1988a) has the same biography. Matthew Price always feels the tension between his father's world—the village to which his father remains loyal despite many temptations and pressures to move out and on—and the wider world of academia. In the end he does not feel comfortable in either.

The tension between going and staying is matched by the pressures on the village itself to change as a result of outside influences. The father (I am still referring to the novel *Border Country*) is involved in the General Strike of 1926 and this brings national and even international politics into the village.

The second novel, *Second Generation* (1988b), looks at the same issues but from the reverse angle. The Welsh villagers have moved to Oxford as there is no work for them in the village. They get employment at the expanding Cowley motor works. The second generation knew Oxford as home, but was it the same sort of home their parents had left behind? In the third novel, *The Fight for Manod* (1988c), the action centres on a plan to turn Manod, a small and frankly insignificant Welsh village, into a New Town with the prospect of major industries moving in, and hundreds of new jobs and houses with them.

All sorts of 'binarisms', to use the postcolonial expression, are thrown up by these novels. There is the universalism of a political credo—socialism in this case—and the particularities of loyalty to family and place. (This also comes up in Williams' fourth novel, *Loyalties* (1999), which begins with a meeting of Welsh miners and Cambridge University students to decide how best to fight fascism in Spain.) There is the clash between town and gown (in *Second Generation*), between town and countryside, between the language of abstraction and the more concrete language of everyday experience, between the 'tourist gaze' and 'lived lives in place', between the horizontal and the vertical.

These tensions are not easily resolved and Williams does not attempt any 'quick fix' in the novels. Nevertheless I feel that he tends quite strongly towards the particularist side of the argument. For one thing he recognises the durability of rooted people and movements. As a good socialist, he worries, for example, about the saying that 'the working man has no country' and wants to re-invent socialism so that the political action of the working-man is embedded in place as much as ideology. As he says,

> Place has been shown to be a crucial element in the bonding process [of the workers...]...by the explosion of the international economy and

> the destructive efforts of deindustrialisation upon old communities. When capital has moved on, the importance of place is more clearly revealed. (Harvey 1996, 29)

Is the same true for Christian communities? In any case, whether we are socialists or Christians or both, I am sure that we would agree with Williams' main point that

> the move from tangible solidarities understood in patterns of social life organised in affective and knowable communities to a more abstract set of conceptions that would have universal purchase involves a move from one level of abstraction—attached to place—to another level of abstraction capable of reaching out across space. (Harvey 1996, 33)

We would also probably agree that something is bound to be lost in this process.

If anything the Kentucky philosopher-farmer Wendell Berry goes even further than Williams. He virtually claims that you cannot lead a fully human life without being 'rooted'. Berry had always believed that his vocation was to be a writer. He secured, as a young man, a teaching post in New York, placing himself, it was generally believed, at the centre of the intellectual life of the nation, precisely where he needed to be if he was to pursue his chosen career. What he must not do, apparently, was to go back to his roots.

There was the belief, long honoured among American intellectuals and artists and writers, that a place such as I came from [rural Kentucky] could be returned to only at the price of intellectual death...(Berry 1981, 78)

Nevertheless he did decide to go back to Kentucky.

What finally freed me from these doubts and suspicions was the insistence in what was happening to me that, far from being bored and diminished or obscured to myself by my life here [back on the farm], I had grown more alive and more conscious than I had ever been. (79)

He continues:

Before coming back I had been willing to allow the possibility—which one of my friends insisted upon—that I already knew this place as well as I ever would. But now I began to see the real abundance and richness of it. It is, I saw, inexhaustible in its history, in the details of its life, in its possibilities. I walked over it, looking, listening, smelling, touching, alive to it as never before. I listened to the talk of my kinsmen and neighbours as I never had done, alert to their knowledge of the place, and to the qualities and energies of their speech. I began more seriously than ever to learn the names of things—the wild plants

> and animals, the natural processes, the local places—and to articulate my observations and memories. (79)

Berry is saying in fact that he not only became a better writer but a better human being. The particular place was a constant source of what might be called 'spiritual nourishment'.

> Though it has come slowly and a little at a time, by bits and fragments sometimes weeks apart, I realise after so many years of just being here that my knowledge of the life of this place is rich, my own life part of that richness. (71)

He fundamentally rejects any idea of parochialism.

> Eternal mysteries are here, and temporal ones too. (71)

Ched Myers has, in some ways, a similar approach to Wendell Berry, only he is more Biblical and theological. He devotes a whole chapter in his book *Who Will Roll Away the Stone?* (Myers 1994, chapter 11) to what he calls 'reclamative theology', in effect an attempt to describe 'The Great Economy', that is to say the Kingdom of God in its twenty first century aspect. He quotes Walter Brueggemann at the outset.

> Radical decisions in obedience are of course the stuff of biblical faith, but now it cannot be radical decisions in a private world without brothers and sisters, without pasts

and futures, without turf to be managed and cherished as a partner in the decisions. The unit of decision-making is the community and that always with reference to the land...The central [biblical] problem is not emancipation but rootage, not meaning but belonging, not separation from community but *location* within it. (336)

Myers' argument is that

Christian theology in pursuit of a universalist doctrine has become not only idealist and abstract but docetic. It must be regrounded in incarnational faith: Immanuel, God among us in this place (377).

Myers, however, does not tackle the New Testament passages which suggest that Christians are by definition 'aliens and exiles' (1 Peter 2:11). Paul speaks about the Philippians as 'citizens of heaven' (Philippians 3:20) , John's Gospel speaks in favour of 'placeless worship' (John 4:21-3) and there is an extended passage in the book of Hebrews which culminates with the idea that the people of faith are 'strangers and foreigners' on the earth (Hebrews 11:13). What do we make of the idea that 'here we have no lasting city' (Hebrews 13:14)? How does this fit in with a 'theology of reclamation'?

I tried out Berry's and Myers' ideas on my academic colleagues. They did not like them at all! On the whole they put very little value on 'place'. No doubt this was partly because they had all spent their lives on the move. Not one of them was now living where they had been brought up, nor did they think this a great loss.

The loss may be there nevertheless. I certainly feel it in my own life. Also the loss may be irreparable. I have been living in the one place (in Gloucester in England) for nearly fifteen years now, but have found it very difficult to connect with the locality. I take daily walks, either in the city itself or in the nearby countryside, and although I enjoy these, there is not really a growing sense that I am more and more at home. Partly this is because my memories of other places—Portugal where I grew up as a boy, Oxford, India—are still very strong, but more importantly because I do not do anything which is significantly local. I do not grow my own food or buy local produce, spend much time in a local pub, support local entertainment (sing in a choir e.g.), or have much interest in local history. Even my work does not now depend much on where I live. My church is not really local either.

Just in case this sounds like the activities of a person who has lost all interest in life, I feel that in some senses I live a very full life. Food and drink is easily and pleasantly obtainable without having to put in much effort. I like red wine, for example, but most of it comes from France! I like Indian cuisine best but have no plans to try and grow the essential ingredients. I do try to patronise the local farmers' market but the choice it offers is fairly limited. I am a consumer of the arts—music, drama, movies—but do not often source these locally, and spend most of my leisure time reading, which again is not context specific. I could do more admittedly on the local history front, though I am turned off by the whole 'heritage industry'. My work takes place at home but has to do mainly with supervising other people's academic work and writing books and articles, and I could do that from anywhere. My church, like most of the churches in the city, is a good place to meet, but has little impact on its local community. If I was forcibly removed to another place, apart from my friends I would lose very little.

In fact, of course, I would be losing very little because I have already lost a great deal. All that binds me into 'place', into the traditions and structures of a particular locality, have already been eroded. In my case this may not be a matter of life and death, but for others it may be little short of that.

Using it as a sort of case study[19], I would like to refer here to the history of a tribal group called the Machiguengas who live in the Peruvian Amazon. In many ways tiny and obscure, the Machiguengas have achieved some fame through Mario Vargas Llosa's novel *El Hablador* (1991). My commentary on the fate of this tribal group is a response to Vargas Llosa's book (I have never been to the Amazon!), and also takes into account a chapter in Benedict Anderson's *The Spectre of Comparisons* (1998). Anderson's chapter, titled *El Malhadado Pais*, is a brilliant meditation on *El Hablador* in the light of his interest in the forms that nationalism have taken in the global South. The title of Vargas Llosa's book refers to its central character, Saúl Zuratas, a Peruvian national, who, through a variety of circumstances, becomes deeply involved with the Machiguengas. So deep is this involvement

19 The following is a summary of an article originally published in *Transformation* (Ingleby 2007).

that he takes to living among them and becomes a *hablador*, someone who journeys from place to place (the tribe is scattered and is characterised by its unwillingness to live in one place or under the authority of one chief) keeping the tribe's history, religion and culture alive, by means of recounting the appropriate stories that make up its self understanding.

The very existence of the Machiguengas is already threatened by their contact with the 'modern' world and it is all the more necessary therefore that they are reminded of their identity. One of the possible threats, at least according to one reading of *El Hablador*, is the work of the Summer Institute of Linguistics (SIL) and its Bible translators. Zuratas, fears the advent of the Gospel, as it is presented by the SIL missionaries, precisely because he sees, or thinks he sees, that the triumph of Christianity will mean the effective passing away of the Machiguengas as a tribe.

And that indeed is the question—a question to do with 'place'. Can we find ways to tell the Christian story that is fully sensitive to context? Would acceptance of that story, for example, necessarily change the relationship of the Machiguengas to the Amazonian jungle? If the taboo system, for example, became otiose could they survive in the jungle? Does this matter? Do we want them to survive as 'jungle people'? Yet the pathos of the situation remains. The very cultural and ethnic diversity, so often celebrated by Christians in terms of Revelation 7:9 is, in terms of Amazonia, in danger of being destroyed by contact with Christianity.

It would seem that Zuratas believes that *any* contact with the outside world is bad for the Machiguengas. But is this the case? Anderson looks at this issue when he relates the office of *hablador* to a passage in the writings of Walter Benjamin about the European *Erzähler* (storyteller) who not only recounts the intimate and 'secret' stories of the community but also brings 'tales from afar'. Typically the *Erzähler* could be either 'itinerants like sailors' or 'rooted residents, such as tillers of the land'. The difficulty with this thesis in terms of the Machiguengas, as Anderson points out (1998, 358), is that the sharing of the 'tales from afar' does not apparently contribute to the *survival* of the Machiguengas. Perhaps after all there is no escape from the predations of modernity and the nation state. That is why Vargas Llosa speaks of Peru as '*el malhadado pais*' (the unfortunate or cursed country). 'Tales from afar' in this case, even if brought by missionaries, turn out to be deadly.

The easy path is simply to say that the Machiguengas have their own history, customs, culture and destiny, and others have theirs, and it is best if the two never meet, certainly best for the Machiguengas. But even in the novel there is overlapping—otherwise there would be no story to tell, only the recital of interesting anthropological phenomena. *El hablador* is in fact not a Machiguenga, he is a half-Jewish *gringo*, Saúl Zuratas. Or to be more exact, the situation portrayed in the novel contains both good and bad overlapping, tragic loss as well as some gain perhaps. I add "perhaps" because Zuratas himself would say that the gains were incomparably meagre. One is reminded of Walter Benjamin's famous dictum, quoted at the head of Benedict Anderson's chapter, 'There is no document of civilisation which is not at the same time a document of barbarism.'

The SIL translators play an important role in the novel if only because Zuratas sees them not just as *an* enemy but *the* enemy (Vargas Llosa 1991, 96-7). The SIL translators were not just Christians but Christians of a particular sort—conservative Evangelical Protestants would be one description. 'Protestant' is important because Protestantism tends to be logocentric (printing presses, preaching, catechisms, education) and of course bibliocentric. The question is: how do you transmit *that sort of Christianity* to the Machiguengas?

This question can be illustrated by another pair of questions. Could Jesus read and write (answer: 'yes') and would it have mattered if he had been illiterate (answer 'no')? Jesus probably knew the Scripture he quoted by heart; he certainly did not carry a copy of the Hebrew Scriptures around with him. Also his teaching was based not on a close exegesis of the text but on stories and aphorisms. He was not a scribe but a *hablador*, somebody who reminded his own people of the stories that made up their history and identity, and reinterpreted them, making them relevant to 'the day and the hour'.

Our whole Western society is logocentric, at least when it comes to formal, official or 'important' communication. It is based on contracts that are legally enforceable and educational qualifications which have primarily to do with reading and writing. Notice that these ways of proceeding are totally useless in the Amazon jungle!

Much could be written about this on either side. It is certainly to the credit of the SIL that they seem to be affirming the identity of the Machiguengas. They are not, for example, turning them into Spanish speakers so that they can more easily integrate into (or more likely serve the purposes of) the nation state and the modern world. The Machiguengas' language is no doubt preserved by the effort to reduce it to writing. By the translation of the Bible there is a further affirmation of that language and an admission that it is possible to use it to name 'the one true God'. From outside the Machiguenga community, people have come who have lived among them and after a lifetime of study have been able to describe and interpret their ways to a wider audience. The most impressive of these people, one must surely admit, are the SIL translators. By empowering tribal groups in the ways mentioned above, as well as by literacy training and primary education, they have made it possible for them to defend themselves against cultural imperialism and even aggressive nationalism. But this may not be the whole story as we have seen. *El hablador* obviously believes that it is precisely the dedication and sensitivity of the SIL missionaries, put to the service of modern ideologies, that render them so dangerous.

In summary, the development that Zuratas greatly feared was that an attempt would be made to integrate the Machiguengas into the modern world, to make them commercially productive, perhaps even to make them feel their connection with Peruvian culture and education. He saw this as a disaster (Vargas Llosa 1991, 96-7). (This is not, as we know, a new idea. Anthropologists and ethnologists have been taking this line for many years.) What interests me about this issue is the further question: is this part of a larger struggle which might be described as the pre-modern taking a stand against the modern, or anti-imperialism, or community against the nation state, or the local against the global, or indeed all of these. Modernity, imperialism, nationalism, globalism—are the Machiguengas up against all these? We may rightly conclude that with such an overpowering force bearing down upon them, they will soon, very soon, cease to exist! Also, in a world that is truly 'globalised' where will they flee, and if they cease from 'walking', as the story movingly portrays, then, at least for them, the sun will fall. In all this the burning, pressing question needs to be asked again: in this unequal contest on which side should the Gospel stand?

Does this mean that I am wholeheartedly in favour of the stance taken by the radical anthropologists? No, not necessarily. In describing the Kingdom of God Jesus does not lay great weight on the significance of ethnic particularity. He was certainly aware of his Jewish heritage, and deeply concerned that the nation should take up its obligations, but for Jesus the basis of God's acceptance was not Jewishness. In defining the true people of God he systematically undermined Jewish particularity (as did the Old Testament prophets and other New Testament teachers). It is not that people's culture, history and ethnicity are unimportant. It is just that in terms of God's rule there are deeper structures, to do with a common acceptance of the Lordship of Christ. The Gospel must be preached to the Machiguengas because, like every other marginalised group, they are the poor to whom the Gospel is particularly directed (Luke 4:18, 7:22). The ultimate question for the Machiguengas, as for every other people, is how can we bring ourselves under the Lordship of Christ. However important their identity as Machiguengas, it is not what defines them as the people of God (Gal 3:28). What would define them as such would be an acceptance of Jesus as Lord.

To return to our main theme, however: there is no doubt that all over the world small communities, local cultures, tribes and peoples are being displaced. It would be idle to deny this, and wrong to ignore it. Wendell Berry perceives this as an important issue for Christians.

Despite its protests to the contrary, modern Christianity has become willy-nilly the religion of the state and the economic status quo. Because it has been so exclusively dedicated to incanting anaemic souls into heaven, it has been made the tool of much earthly villainy. It has, for the most part, stood silently by while a predatory economy has ravaged the world, destroyed its natural beauty and health, divided and plundered its human communities and households. It has flown the flag and chanted the slogans of empire. It has assumed with the economists that 'economic forces' automatically work for good and has assumed with the industrialists and militarists that technology determines history. It has assumed with almost everybody that 'progress' is good, that it is good to be modern and up with the times. It has admired Caesar and comforted him in his depredations and defaults. (Berry 1993, 114-5)

Environment: the 'green' context

This attack on the life-worlds of indigenous peoples, just described, has serious environmental consequences. If only for that reason, in the current political and economic climate, localities need to be defended. But this is not just in the Global South. If we are all being abstracted from our social context and falling out of love with 'place' then I suspect that nothing will save us from what we see now—*the systematic destruction of our environment.*

Even a 'modern' nation is not exempt. Paul Kingsnorth in his excellent book *Real England* (2008) shows very clearly that if we do not come to the defence of what he calls 'real England' it will be wiped out by a combination of big business (working with government) and the wealthy urban bourgeoisie. (He also wants to say that it will be our fault 'because of our reluctance to discuss who and what we are as a nation or to stand up for our places, our national character and our cultural landscape' (13). We have fallen out of love with the local and it is what we love that we defend.)

I have just been reading an article on the relationship between Critical Theory and our attitude to the environment. It says nothing about the importance of 'the local' and yet it is very relevant to what I have just written. Thus:

> Sociological analysis of environmental problems, therefore [i.e. because of the preceding argument based on the interpretation of Critical Theory] has to be closely linked to a comprehensive and historically reflected social theory from which nature…may not be excluded. On the other hand, we have to take into account that… the natural can never be 'extracted from its societal form' (Adorno in Wehling 2002, 162-3)

What does this mean? I think it probably means that we are doomed. My mind goes back to a recent conference I attended on environmental issues. It was held, through no fault of its own, at a time when the economic crisis was at its most menacing. The chairperson kicked off by saying that, as the economic system was so evidently crashing, it was a good opportunity to get a new one which would give us a chance of ecological survival. An extremely distinguished delegate from DIFID (the first speaker in fact) immediately intervened to say that this was precisely not what was required. Indeed it was 'by-path meadow' of the first order to discuss 'the economic system'. What was needed was for men and women of good will (the implication being that we were those people—how flattering!) to be sure that when growth resumed, and even before then, that the economy was raided for the necessary resources to initiate technological change. In terms of the quotation above, this meant a 'scientific' solution was 'in', but a social theory was 'out'. All that was required was an adjustment. The economic crisis was a regrettable interlude because it meant that less money was available for the necessary technological innovations.

But no! This 'strenuous extraction of the natural from its societal form', the divorce of the science of nature from its political, economic and cultural matrix will lead, as I say, directly to environmental disaster. There are, in fact, no solutions to human dilemmas without due consideration of the human condition. The example given in the article cited (161) is the automobile industry. We can create an energy-saving car, but can we create a society which is freed from the addiction to motoring, or the need for the car, the van and the lorry as essential commercial means to maintain our way of life?

The environmental crisis is another example of the problematic economics introduced by globalisation. Obviously the crisis is truly global in the sense that we are all contributing to it (some more than others, however) and will all bear its effects. Global warming has taken over the mantle of nuclear proliferation as 'mutually assured destruction'. The key is that we cannot opt out. What is happening on the other side of the globe affects us. Similarly, if we are going to find a solution, it will have to be done on a global scale. We look at our fragile earth and realise that the planet itself is under threat. Visions of the planet from outer space remind us not only of its smallness and isolation, but that 'we are all in the same boat now'. At least for the time being we have nowhere else to go, and if this is indeed the case then we must simply stop doing harmful things to our habitat. If you are heading for a cliff, stop the car, turn around and drive off in a different direction (Goldsmith 2001, 13).

It is not just that we need to take seriously the various doom-laden evaluations of our environmental future (see most powerfully Kovel 2002). The whole situation is vitally linked to the issues of distribution and security. So often the missing jewel of our conversation about environmentalism is justice. Old Testament writers were careful to include it. They celebrated the justice of Yahweh and prayed that they might experience it because they knew that only then would they and the nations round about really know prosperity (Psalm 67:4-6). It was simply not possible to have one without the other.

Environmental degradation, at least in part, is a product of systematic exploitation, and that in two senses of the word. The earth is being exploited and people are being exploited. The latter leads to poverty which in turn leads to bad news for the environment. Obviously the quest for unrestrained wealth and its enjoyment leads to extravagance and waste. Gas-guzzling cars might be a simple example. On the other side, poor people do not drive big cars but poor people, too, can be wasteful. Often they simply cannot afford to live in an ecologically friendly way. If you need firewood from the forest to cook your evening meal you do not stop to ask whether you are contributing to deforestation.

Why is that Christians, of all people, seem so indifferent to this situation? (There are noble exceptions, of course, such as the John Ray Initiative.) I suppose it may have something to do with our reading of cosmic history. The popularity of the Tim La Haye series in the United States comes into the picture here. The first difficulty can be crudely expressed thus: if the end of the world is just around the corner who cares about the environment? If Scripture teaches that the whole house is going to go up in smoke why bother to rearrange the furniture? In fact a careful reading of Romans 8 and 1 Peter 3 suggests that this is not the case, and that it is God's plan to renew the creation rather than destroy it. I believe that the present preoccupation with Biblical apocalyptic is a troubling development. It diverts us from giving the apocalyptic passages in the Bible their true worth—essentially a call to justice rather than a timetable for the future. Sadly, the futurists, with their supposedly Biblical basis, find ready allies among the wealthy and powerful (sometimes they are the same people) who have a vested interest in keeping the world's economic system working as it does at present, and disregarding environmental warnings[20].

Community and government

An important part of the culture that forms our context is our community. The fact is that community offers huge benefits. Communities may be under attack today—as we have suggested in our study of 'place' and 'environment'—but few would seriously suggest that we can do without them! Indeed, given that the nation state does not command the loyalty it once did, and that globalisation seems to be sweeping away many familiar landmarks, community tends to be the refuge into which we retreat. This is a two edged sword. Loyalty to the community and solidarity with my cultural heritage, while clearly good things

20 See again Ingleby 2010b.

in themselves, are also, because of their inherent power and universal appeal, forces which very easily become demonic—a product we sometimes call 'communalism'.

Communalism is the tendency of men and women to put ultimate confidence in their own human traditions. It is as widespread as humankind itself. Historically it has usually taken a religious form, not so much individual spirituality as religious community law. The law of the community demands piety, which in turns involves a respect for custom, a thoughtful observance of appropriate ritual (the ritual itself is a sort of public demonstration of traditional values) veneration of parents and ancestors, and above all moral rectitude and uprightness. Piety of this sort is in fact not very common, and in some cases may be the result of a life-long search for God. As the apostle Paul says, 'Some people keep on doing good, and seek glory, honour and immortal life; to them God will give eternal life' (Romans 2:7).

However, equally often piety is not an attempt to seek after God, but to exclude him, and in this case the law of the community is generally given divine sanction and becomes the ultimate goal. God, so to speak, is called in to add his authority to the arrangements. Many a man or woman has suffered at the hands of their own community and been named a rebel against God, when at most they are guilty of impiety and more probably just do not know the rules. We see examples of this in Arthur Miller's *The Crucible*.

For legalism (as we might call it) has two faces. It can be a heart-breaking attempt to win God's favour by our good behaviour and it can be an attempt to enforce our rules on others in order to justify the goals that we have made autonomous. A spin-off of this second attitude is self-righteousness. If you define your objectives in a carefully circumscribed manner and attain them, then it is also important that you magnify your achievement, perhaps by downgrading those who have tried and failed to follow the same path. The Pharisee in the Temple (Luke 18:9-14) had to point out his religious achievements, and was equally compelled to compare himself favourably with the tax-collector. What happens when somebody comes along and says that your rule-keeping is not enough ("unless your righteous deeds exceed those of the Scribes and Pharisees you will not enter the Kingdom of Heaven") is another story. If possible you have them put away.

The parable of the Pharisee and the tax-collector puts the whole affair in a very individual way. This man, thinks the Pharisee, is, as it were, an outcaste as far as my values are concerned. But we have already seen that this derives from and adds fuel to community actions and reactions. For the community as well as for individuals the opposite of law (in the sense of legalism) is grace. Paul knew very well what he was doing when he made these two opposites and resisted any definition of the Gospel which ignored this sharply drawn antithesis. The point is this: grace is by definition an exception to the rule and laws can allow no exception and remain law. A community which is defined by its rules is already ceasing to be a community if it allows anyone—even God—to dispense with these rules.

Paul, in a famous passage, describes how he has kept the rules: he had the right entrance ticket (circumcision) and the right credentials (very important this: clubs to be clubs have to be exclusive) and 'as far as a person can be righteous by obeying the commands of the Law, I was without fault', but something else came into his experience which made these things seem to be worthless to him by comparison (Philippians 3: 4b-11). Now quite apart from the question as to whether what Paul had got—the grace of God in Jesus Christ—was more important than what he had left behind, it seems indubitable that Paul had resigned from the club. All the rules were now inoperative for him and if enough people took the same attitude the club itself would cease to exist.

Again, it is important to stress that this is not just a question of the Jews. We have a splendidly amusing incident in Acts 19 (not so funny, no doubt, if you were actually involved in it) when Paul and his companions got into trouble with the pagan silversmiths at Ephesus. Demetrius, the instigator of the trouble, is a hard-headed business-man. Any attack on the city's idolatry was an attack on the livelihood of himself and his colleagues. 'Men, you know that our prosperity comes from this work,' he says. This reminds us that a community means institutions and that these in turn mean jobs, status, security and so on. Demetrius then continues, 'There is a danger, then, that this business of ours will get a bad name. Not only that, but there is also the danger that the temple of the great goddess Artemis will come to mean nothing and that her greatness will be destroyed—the goddess worshipped by everyone in Asia and in all the world!' Quite right, Demetrius, quite right. Who worships Artemis now?

And the town clerk who was doing his best to keep the peace, like the conscientious civil servant he undoubtedly was, was quite wrong. 'Everyone knows that the city of Ephesus is the keeper of the temple of the great Artemis and of the sacred stone that fell down from heaven. Nobody can deny these things... There is no excuse for all this uproar and we should not be able to give a good reason for it.' In fact there was every excuse for the uproar and Demetrius had given a perfectly good reason for it. Anyone who thinks that communal riots have no rationale has learnt nothing from history. If anyone thinks so still let him go and live in Kashmir or Northern Ireland or Sri Lanka or Brixton.

In brief, a community is defined by its rules. The unexpectedness, the outsidedness, the otherness of God's grace is inevitably a threat to communalism. Many cannot accept this break with the rules. We see this in the life of Gandhi. Religion *must* consist primarily of ethical behaviour (rules) otherwise it ceases to exist entirely. As Terence Rynne has put it:

> He [Gandhi] found the life and message of Jesus very attractive but he resisted the Christian's way of describing salvation, unable to understand how a person could be saved all in one go by calling on someone else for salvation. (2008, 9)

The confrontation between law and grace can be described in a different way as ethics versus eschatology. One of the reasons why Jesus' preaching presented an immediate threat to the Jewish establishment was that it was thoroughly eschatological in character. 'Repent,' said Jesus, 'the Kingdom of God is at hand'. Something is 'blowing in the wind'. Something is just around the corner, something is coming next, which is so cataclysmic that it will blow your carefully contrived structures into little pieces. You people who are carefully adjusting your rules to make it possible for you to live under Roman rule and to be a good Jew at the same time, look out, the King is coming, indeed he may be here already in disguise, about to set up his kingdom and who is to say that *you* will be the beneficiaries? Ethical behaviour is certainly required, but of the sort that is appropriate to the new age which is about to dawn.

We read that the common people heard Jesus gladly. After all the old rules had been drawn up in such a way as to exclude them. Perhaps when the new age dawned, by some miracle, they would be inside after all. If I may draw a modern analogy, in 1914 when the First World War broke out, the event provoked or was the result of an eschatological ferment similar to that which we can observe in Jesus' day. In every capital of Europe the announcement of war led to enthusiastic, not to say delirious, scenes. It seems unlikely that the prospect of war itself produced this enthusiasm. But there was another prospect. The old structured Europe with its carefully drawn rules, its privileged classes, its haves and its have-nots, was now at risk. The roof had blown off and everybody was now in the open and anything could happen. Thus it is that eschatology, true or false, threatens the system, and the 'system' as far as communities are concerned, is what it is all about. It follows therefore that communalism needs to express its aspirations in terms which are non-eschatological.

What does this mean in practice? Well, usually it means the promise of, and if possible the achievement of, the prosperous life. Communalism is basically materialistic. It is a philosophy suitable for 'haves'. 'You never had it so good' is its motto, and the inference is, so why bother to change? Further, it is ethical behaviour (obeying the rules) that produces prosperity. Certain elements in the Old Testament (and in the New Testament for that matter: we may notice the disciples' astonishment when Jesus said that it was difficult for a rich man to enter the Kingdom) favoured this approach. So does today's 'prosperity Gospel'.

Part of the debate surrounding community and communalism is its relation to the nation state. Does the fact that we belong to a particular nation really make that much difference? For many Christians the response may be a shrug of the shoulders. This is the least of our problems. The question as to whether Westminster, or equivalent, hangs on to its power seems rather remote. Further we feel that the mission of the church is not really called into question by this debate...and it is at this point that doubts should begin to gather. The shape of the world has always mattered to those involved in the mission of the church, and the shape of the world is a political question.

So does the nation matter and if so how should we define it? Half a century ago, or thereabouts, the idea of a world comprised of 'nations' was not one that was much contested. There were Empires of course—British, French, Dutch, Portuguese—but they were in the process of being dismantled. The inheritors were to be the new nation states, such as India, Ghana, and Indonesia, and anti-imperialism and nationalism went hand in hand. Perhaps nobody foresaw the extent to which these nation states and other older ones, were to come under pressure from within. Yet the truth is that the whole idea of the nation state appears to be 'up for grabs' today. Certainly questions are being asked. Is the nation state necessary to modernity? Is it a friend or enemy of culture and ethnicity? Why does it create such obvious loyalty? Should it? How do we distinguish nationalism (bad) from patriotism (good)? Indeed what is the nation in the first place?

Anthony Smith has some interesting ideas here (Smith A 1995). He introduces three descriptions of nationalism, all of which have considerable power. They are:

- Nations and nationalisms are the survivals of an epoch now about to pass away. The chariot of progress is in fact hitched to such structures as 'the international division of labour, great regional markets, powerful military blocs, electronic communications, computerised information technology, mass public education, the mass media, the sexual revolution and the like'(3). Nationalism as an autonomous political force has had its day.

- Nations and nationalism are inevitable products, and producers, of modernity. They are the absolutely necessary instruments for controlling the massive social changes that modernity has introduced. Nationalism as an ideology is the only successful means of validation of the modern state, and for this reason neither the ideology nor the state itself is likely to disappear, at least until an affluent and stable modernity on the Western model has become universal.

• Nations and nationalism are perennial, almost a fact of nature. The ethnic community and the nation are 'essential building blocks of any conceivable order' at any point in history (5).

Smith considers that none of these descriptions does justice to underlying ethnic and territorial contexts. To understand nations 'we must set them in the wider historical intersection between cultural ties and political communities'. We need a long timeframe and a recovery of 'the ethnic substratum' to do the job of description properly. (An example, I would suggest, though not one given by Smith, would be the revival of Welsh nationalism.)

> Nations are linked by the chains of memory, myth and symbol to that widespread and enduring type of community, the *ethnie*, and this is what gives them their unique character and their profound hold over the feelings and imaginations of so many people. (159)

Smith here is re-presenting a debate which is far from over. Is the state losing its grip, and, if so, is this a good thing or not? Many feel that the nation *has already been discarded* as a primary source of loyalty and motivation. There are new sources of loyalty both above and below the nation, so to speak. Bigger than the nation (in terms of loyalty) might be, for some, God, or 'development' or the multi-national I work for. At the other end of the spectrum a deeper loyalty may exist for my family, or my community, for personal friends or for my own career. An Indian friend of mine once remarked that 'there are very few Indians in India'. What he meant was that there were plenty of Tamilians or Gujeratis or Bengalis, and this affiliation was much more important to them than their national identity.

I suggest that the nation finds it increasingly difficult to command *undivided* loyalty. Who does Capello want to win when England plays Italy at football? More seriously, what do I do when my government attacks or undermines my religion? Why were (are?) British and American nationals fighting on the Taliban side in Afghanistan? In what sense was an American fighting against the USA when he was fighting against the Northern Alliance? More importantly what appeal were these people making to an overriding religious loyalty and is this not something that we Christians should be interested in? 'We must obey God rather than men' has a familiar ring to it. In short, the 'mixed' situation has become a commonplace of our world, and questions of loyalty are becoming more complex, not less so.

Another question is whether the state *can* control its own future. It seems certain to me that the state, though not by any means ready to wither away, is becoming increasingly unable to withstand certain pressures. The carefully constructed boundaries that have previously defined the state are being crossed with increasing ease. Thus, many wealthy states are making huge efforts to keep out illegal drugs. Apparently, they are simply not able to do so.

Again, if the state cannot deliver what its citizens demand, it will have to look to outside help to do so. The Kingdom of Nepal, for example, for many years wanted both to remain somewhat impervious to outside influences, particularly any that was undermining of its status as a Hindu nation, but at the same time wanted to introduce its people to the positive factors associated with modernity—education, health care, better agriculture and the like. Yet it found that it could not have it both ways. It could not deliver the latter without the help of those who in effect forced it to give up its isolation.

To put it another way, the state is a 'container', a political space defined in terms of national territorial boundaries. Within those boundaries the state exercises a number of powers, for example the right to use legitimate force. The difficulty is that increasingly the walls of the container are porous.

> Goods, capital, knowledge, ideas and weapons, as well as crime, pollutants, fashions and micro-organisms readily move across national territorial boundaries.
> (Held & McGrew 2000, 135)

Also it is not just that there is an increasing volume of global exchange and cross-border activity but it has been necessary to match this with numerous organisations, governmental and non-governmental, in order to manage this process. Some power has necessarily been ceded to these organisations. Even more alarmingly, modern states are finding that decisions made outside their boundaries, over which they have no control, increasingly affect the lives of their citizens. For example, states can no longer effectively control the transnational flow of information. All sorts of messages, using a variety of sophisticated technologies, cross their borders and there is little chance that these can be successfully intercepted or controlled. What happens by means of the Internet is a particularly good example. Attempts to control its use are bound to be made in the future, but with what success? There are big issues at stake here. Many historians now feel, for example, that the fall of the Soviet bloc was achieved not so much by military pressure, but by the sheer impossibility of the Soviet bloc continuing to live in isolation from its wealthier neighbours.

Examples of this are everywhere. Can states de-link themselves from the big financial players, such as the International Monetary Fund and the World Trade Organisation, and prosper? What about the way that capital moves around the world, irrespective of the needs of governments? Equally, Trans National Corporations have diversified their operations to such an extent that they do not really have a base in any one country. On the political front, co-operation and networking are also crucial. There is a growing feeling that human rights should be enforced on some world-wide basis, that an individual government cannot simply treat people badly, even if they are its own people, and be allowed to get away with it. When the time comes for intervention that too needs to be a co-operative enterprise (Held & McGrew 1999, 68). Even the US, 'the world's most powerful nation' has found that it needs allies in its military adventures.

All this is a matter of considerable tension. Having bought into 'internationalism', national governments find that they do not necessarily like the consequences. Take the idea of international justice, for example. Are we in Britain grateful that we have a European Court or do we feel that its rulings are 'interference'? Why, we may ask, is the US so opposed to the idea of an international court which can try 'world criminals' such as those guilty of crimes against humanity?

Is the nation state then losing its grip entirely as far as loyalty is concerned? You might judge so from the above, but I doubt it. Consider, for example, the outpouring of patriotic fervour evoked by 9/11 in the USA. Again, why are Pakistan and India so much at loggerheads over Kashmir? Both governments know well that they can play 'the nation in danger' card and evoke huge support. For a country so divided in terms of race, ethnicity, language, customs and religion it is surprisingly easy to unite Indians by an appeal to nationalism. Some sort of identity has certainly been constructed here. And if a state 'enjoys legitimacy as a result of the loyalty and consent of its citizens' (Held & McGrew 2000, 9) then India is in business. Yet complexity remains. What are the true feelings, I wonder, of Indian Muslims separated from their relatives in Pakistan, and increasingly aware that India is influenced by Hindu nationalism?

In fact the nation state can still do much for us. Here are some suggestions.

• The state can defend people against the bad effects of globalisation. Politically, global institutions still suffer from what is called the 'democratic deficit'. Economically the state has, in cases such as Britain, Germany, France, Sweden etc., been the means whereby economic wealth has been fairly apportioned. Who will fairly administer the distribution of education, health care and pensions if the state does not do so?

• The state can provide a forum for inter-ethnic, inter-tribal disputes. These are not new and the state may be a mechanism for containing strife, as in the former Yugoslavia, or, perhaps, in present day South Africa.

• In terms of mission the state may provide an umbrella for cross-cultural evangelism and church planting, as in India.

It follows that there are a number of international commentators who feel that the increasing weakness of the state is overall a bad thing. Frederic Jameson, (Jameson 2000) for example, believes that nationalism ought not to be allowed to perish; it can be partially revived and used to resist any future attempts at imperialism or economic globalisation. This would involve a new nationalist politics, a benign sort which transcends the limited goal of national independence and power. He admits that there is a sort of malign nationalism which merely creates border wars (like those within the former Yugoslavia); benign nationalism, by contrast, has, as part of its constitutive behaviour, resistance to the system, in this case to US led globalisation. We might call this a sort of Gaullism. Apart from a few mass protests (Seattle, Genoa etc.)

Jameson believes that the site of this resistance may have to continue to be the nation state itself, as it seeks to defend such features of its life as labour protection laws, national cultures (an example would be the French film industry) welfare legislation, patent laws and so on.

Jameson admits that it is not clear that nationalism in and by itself can be an adequate weapon against globalisation, if only because it suffers from the fatal philosophical flaw, identified by Partha Chatterjee, that it is trying to universalise a particular. Let nationalist passion, in the Gaullist sense, (can we call this 'patriotism'?) be the driving force, and let the battle be partially fought on national issues but something more will be needed, namely 'a genuinely universalistic opposition'. 'After the disappearance of the internationalist Communist movement it would seem that, on the world stage, only certain currents within Islam—generally characterised as 'fundamentalist'—really position themselves in programmatic opposition to Western culture, or certainly to Western 'cultural imperialism'. From a Christian point of view this may mean that it is time for us to get busy! Are we really abandoned to a choice between secularism and Islam as the only two possible world views?

But to return to the nation state: for every argument in favour of it there is one against.

• The state itself can be the agent of rampant global capitalism, as when it enters into deals with multinationals at the expense of its own people, for example logging in Malaysia (Allen &

Thomas 1992, 109-110) or the extraction of oil by Shell in Nigeria (Maier 2000 chapter 4).

• It can exacerbate inter-tribal and inter-ethnic conflicts, particularly when there is a perceived majority/minority situation.

• State borders have often been used to keep missionaries out. Nationalism has been consistently used as an ideology to exclude the message of the Gospel. Christianity has been seen as a 'non-Indian religion', for example.

• The belief that the nation demands our unquestioned loyalty has produced all sorts of idolatrous and tragic situations, such as two world wars.

This is only a very brief list. There are many who simply see the supposed demise of the nation state as a good thing, though not necessarily for the reasons above. There are those who see the state as having a very limited and specific role: 'holding the door' for worldwide processes of economic expansion linked to world trade and better communications, and then retiring. There are those who would agree that there is no going back to the pre-eminence of the nation state, but who want to go forward to a new sort of globalisation which is not tied to capitalism. Michael Hardt and Antonio Negri's book *Empire* (Hardt & Negri 2000) is particularly interesting in this respect.

Where do Christians stand in this debate? The nation state still has very considerable significance for us, I suspect, particularly in an era of globalisation. We cannot easily dispense in our missiology, for example, with the idea of the nation, linked as it is to ethnicity and having, as it does, 'a profound hold over the feelings and imaginations', (Anthony Smith's words—see above) of so many. This would be to vote for dehumanising people. No doubt sometimes the nation has a less tenacious grip on people's loyalty, and where this is the case, it may be that they have grounded their identities elsewhere. But where the nation still commands people's loyalty it may still be a necessary and useful ally in the struggle against Empire, as it has been in the past.

Part of the problem in assessing a Christian response is that, as we have seen, the nation state itself has more than one aspect. Let me re-cap some of my arguments. Benign nationalism has to do with attempts to construct or support a nation because of the value of its tradition—its history, culture, language and so on. We Christians should be in favour of this. Malign nationalism, on the other hand, is simply an attempt to seize the state and create a 'power', with the nation usually defined against other nations ('my country, right or wrong'). It is also a sort of tribalism or communalism writ large. Christians should have nothing to do with this sort of thing. It leads directly to all sorts of fanaticism and oppression, often in the name of religion. In India, for example, we currently have parties, such as the BJP, that appeal to nationalism (just as Adolf Hitler did in Germany in the 1930s) but the nation they imagine excludes Muslims and other 'minorities', indeed the 'nation' is defined mostly in terms of religion ('*Hindu* nationalism') something which has been largely eschewed in Europe since the end of the wars of religion and the coming of the Enlightenment.

In truth we Christians are rather muddled in the way that we think about all this. We have a real regard for the ideals of the secular state, which supposedly holds the ring so that all religions have the freedom to flourish. The United States of America was famously founded on this basis, though the impulse behind these novel arrangements was again the European Enlightenment and the fear of religious conflict. (Ironically, many Indians also pride themselves on being members of a secular state, an idea that Nehru and the other founding fathers borrowed from European socialism.) Yet American Christians are keen to think of themselves as part of a Christian civilisation, indeed of a Christian nation (though presumably not a Christian state). There is a considerable tension here, one which we have lived with for a long time in the UK, where we still have a monarchy which, theoretically at least, is a Christian institution, not to mention an established Church, and Christian schools subsidised by the state. When these arrangements are challenged, particularly by another religion such as Islam, our response is confused. Even my question as to how Christians are going to respond when the choice seems one between secularism and Islam is not an easy one to answer. Does this mean more Christian laws? What are they? Does it mean more Christian institutions? Does it mean Christians having more of a 'voice' in public affairs? Should we support Christian communities as such in those numerous parts of the world where they are in bitter conflict against Muslims?

If community is too narrow a way to think about our 'political' context, and the nation state is increasingly a relic of modernity, what about global government? For example, are we about to see a new *Pax Romana*? Certainly there is a growing body of international law. The UN Declaration of Human Rights (1948) and subsequent conventions have, more or less, adopted the idea that the world community has the right to try and stop a government acting in contravention of human rights even if the people it is treating badly are its own people. The idea of an international court—not yet fully realised—follows this idea through.

In fact there is an increasing incidence of international intervention. Kossovo and East Timor are examples of the power of international bodies (NATO, the United Nations, the IMF) to impose their wills on nations and regions. People are talking about a world society even if a world government seems well out of reach. Similarly, cries for help in situations of natural disaster are addressed to the international community. 'Cries for help' are something which Christian mission is equipped to hear, but mission, too, must be *international* in its response, not focussed on narrow ethnic considerations.

Can we have good global society *and* healthy local action? As we have seen, at some levels globalisation allows the 'little people' into a measure of power. Almost anyone nowadays can have a web site of their own and the electronic media can be used not only to spread but to subvert economic globalisation. A sense that we must, in global matters too, act for ourselves and that we cannot leave governments to act on our behalf has led to a increasing number of International Non Government Organisations (INGOs) many of which are now household names[21]. Though globalisation may have contributed to the trend by which people are alienated from traditional politics, it is also true that many more are involved in special interest groups, and want their voices to be heard when they speak about them, indeed some of the most powerful political and economic action today stems from the operation of special interest groups (Greens, the 'disabled' lobby, Campaign Against the Arms Trade etc.). Many Christian organisations have always operated on this basis. (Jubilee 2000 was a notable example.) No doubt there are further possibilities.

Thus Christians cannot afford to ignore politics of this sort. People, according to Anthony Giddens, are more politically minded than they used to be, not less so. They may be suspicious of politics as currently on offer, but younger people, in particular, see such issues as ecological questions, human rights, family policy and sexual freedom as highly significant. They are not sure what the nation state can do about this, and they therefore tend to put their energies into these special interest groups (Giddens 1999, 74-5). Giddens response to this situation is that we need to 'democratise democracy' (75). He wants political parties to learn to collaborate with single-issue groups (Jubilee 2000 is again a good example).

In Britain, 20 times more people belong to voluntary or self-help groups than are members of political parties. (77)

21 For example, Amnesty International, Médicins sans Frontières, Oxfam

The 'little people agendas' mentioned above are part of this. The web-site and the internet allow us all to have a say, as does the ubiquitous phone-in. We are, if we want to be, better informed because of global communications, and therefore it is more difficult for the authorities to hide things away in dark corners. There are documentaries about everything, and unethical companies with headquarters in the wealthy world are held to account by television trial for their misdeeds in the remotest parts of the earth.

So we have two trends. Globalisation speaks initially of large scale operations: centralised institutions like the United Nations or an international court, and a network in which there are powerful controllers. However globalisation produces a reaction, particularly because of its ability to threaten small communities and this has led, politically, to increasing importance being placed on acting locally. Regionalism, local government, subsidiarity (the idea that decisions are best taken by those who have to implement them, or by those upon whom the greatest weight of the outcome will fall) are all important and popular political ideas at the moment. The bigger the world we inhabit the more we feel we need to control the local and familiar. In local politics the neighbourhood man or woman who has established a reputation, particularly for trustworthiness, is often more than a match for the representatives of the big political parties. There remains in our political behaviour a fundamental split between the genuine attraction of being part of 'the big picture' and on the other hand believing that the best decisions for 'our place' are made by 'our folk'. Frankly, 'the big bad world' can cause a good deal of stress. Our political world appears in turns irrelevant or threatening, 'an automated random sequence of events, derived from the uncontrollable logic of markets, technology, geopolitical order, or biological determination', as Castells has rather brilliantly put it (Castells 2000, 508).

This tension between the local and the global has been described in a number of ways. Benjamin Barber, famously, has characterised the key struggle of our age in terms of 'Jihad versus McWorld' (Lechner & Boli 2000, 21-6). The world presents a choice, apparently, between 'the market's universal church' and 'a retribalising politics of particularist identities'. What falls through the middle is the democratic nation. Everyone is a consumer; everyone belongs to some tribe; nobody is a citizen.

> Antithetical in every detail, Jihad and McWorld nonetheless conspire to undermine our hard won (if only half won) civil liberties.

The two are in symbiotic relationship.

> Jihad not only revolts against but abets McWorld, while McWorld not only imperils but re-creates and reinforces Jihad. (26)

In simple terms, both Jihad and McWorld are going on at the same time, both are reacting to the other and also producing the other. The casualties are the nation state and democracy.

Samuel Huntingdon in his '*The Clash of Civilisations*' (Lechner & Boli 2000, 27-33) suggests that at the heart of the conflict is not so much modern versus pre-modern but a clash of *civilisations* and this will dominate global politics henceforth. The period between the Peace of Westphalia and the end of the Cold War (1648-1990) was characterised in the West by civil wars between princes, nations and ideologies. But ideology politics have given way to identity politics. The centrepiece of international politics will be, henceforth, the interaction between Western and non-Western civilisations. (Huntingdon distinguishes seven or eight different civilisations: Western, Confucian (Chinese), Japanese, Islamic, Hindu, Slavic-Orthodox (Russian), Latin American and possibly African.)

He is convinced that this will be the case because cultural divisions are basic or fundamental in the way that no others are. Political and economic differences are relatively easy to transcend. Cultural ones are more stubborn. For example, Europe can create economic unity on the basis of a common European culture but Japan or China will find it much more difficult to 'unite' South East Asia. Also the world is becoming smaller and interactions are more frequent. People are moving more (usually for economic reasons) and are therefore being separated from their 'original' identities. Loss of identity allows fundamentalisms to move in to fill the gap. At the very same time that the mass of the people are being 'Westernised' by means of cultural globalisation, non-Western elites are 'going back to roots'.

Huntingdon suggests a number of fault lines between civilisations, e.g. between the eastern boundary of Western Christianity (stabilised circa 1500) and the Orthodox or Islamic peoples to the East and the South. The conflict between the West and Islam is of course very high profile at the moment, but, says Huntingdon, we forget that it has been going on for 1300 years. In some ways, despite the seven or eight civilisations, the biggest fault line remains the West versus the Rest.

> Western ideas of individualism, liberalism, constitutionalism, human rights, equality, liberty, the rule of law, democracy, free markets, the separation of church and state, often have little resonance in Islamic, Confucian, Japanese, Hindu, Buddhist or Orthodox cultures. (33)

Finally—we are still following Huntingdon here— the conflict between the West and the Rest has already taken three forms. Some, like North Korea and Myanmar have simply attempted to isolate themselves from Western influence. Others have made a strenuous attempt to join the West, accepting its values and institutions. A third group has wanted to modernise but not Westernise while at the same time joining with others who want to do the same to resist the West. They have found this difficult, however.

The West needs to realise that others are not going to become essentially like them even if they are modernising. The West's greatest need is to understand this and to learn to live in 'a world of different civilisations, each of which will have to learn to coexist with the others' (33).

I confess I am not entirely convinced by Huntingdon's thesis. It is all too easy to 'essentialise' civilisations in this way. Despite civilisational differences I detect a global culture in the offing. However, Huntingdon is right in stressing that this will not be achieved except through much conflict.

For Christians much of this conflict, this 'clash of civilisations', is expressed through the perceived rise of Islam. People are aware that there is some sort of Christian-Muslim confrontation going on, but they are not clear what attitudes they should have to this. Are Muslims now being shown in their true colours, and is this a chance to speak up for those, like many Christians, who are being persecuted by Muslim governments (think of southern Sudan, Indonesia, Pakistan)? In areas where the Muslims and Christians are vying for power, particularly in sub-Saharan Africa, there is a similar feeling: 'now we see what Muslims are really like, and what we Christians are up against'. Even in the West there are those who view with disquiet what they consider to be the growing influence of Islam.

Other Christians want to be more careful. They sympathise with those who have religious motivation and are prepared to give Muslims the benefit of the doubt when they give rather confused signals. After all, we have our extremists too. We do not wish to adopt the secularist standpoint that religion is the cause of all our troubles, nor the view that ultimately religion is not the issue.

Our 'balanced' position as Christians, our refusal to demonise 'the enemy' and to take sides does not mean that we can do nothing. I am going to suggest a number of actions which I believe would be appropriate for Christians.

- We need more history, more geography, more politics, in a word more understanding. For example, are we aware that Muslims feel deeply threatened by the (Christian) West? After all they have been on the back foot for almost a couple of centuries. So how can we de-threaten them? Also have we got the right story? We think that Islam is on the march, but as Edward Said has said,

> What appears in the West to be the emergence, return to, or resurgence of Islam is in fact a struggle in Islamic societies over the definition of Islam. (Said 2003, 333)

- The present crisis may be an opportunity for getting to know Muslims in the locality. I was involved in a number of protests against the wars in Afghanistan and Iraq, and was surprised at the easy way this brought me into contact with Muslims in the community. We did not always agree, but at least we were on the same platform. But we must show that we are genuinely interested in what they are interested in.

- Perhaps it has never occurred to us that many Muslims are as disturbed by terrorism as we are. After all they are getting blamed for it, even when they have lived exemplary lives as citizens and are supporters of law and order. Surely this presents an opportunity for us Christians to reassure them on these occasions.

• We need a *distinctive* Christian voice. There may be an opportunity to disentangle ourselves from the misunderstandings that so often go along with the word 'Christian', particularly among Muslims.

If we Christians care, and really want to prove to our neighbours that we are fair minded people, somewhat delivered from the 'special pleading' that annoys us so much when other communities do it to us, why have we not protested more vigorously about, for example, the treatment of the prisoners taken in the war in Afghanistan? Most of these are, perhaps, Taliban and Al Qaeda prisoners, but the cavalier disregard of their legal rights is simply another example of the United States administration acting outside of the law in the spirit of 'might is right'. The Taliban soldiers, for example, are the same soldiers that the United States supported in the war against the Russians during the time of the Russian invasion. There was no talk then of the illegality of their struggle. Jimmy Carter's national security adviser, Zbigniew Brezinski, let slip in an interview with *Le Nouvel Observateur* that the US began aiding the Afghan *mujahedin* six months before the 1979 Soviet invasion. 'That secret operation was an excellent idea,' said Brezinski in 1998. 'It had the effect of drawing the Russians into the Afghan trap, and you want me to regret it?' In other words the Taliban, Al Qaeda et al. are America's gift to the world [22].

Furthermore, in the recent war how can the United States administration be sure that they have got the right men? In the confusion of the sort of

22 See *New Statesman* 14 January, 2002, p. 50

war that was waged in Afghanistan is it not possible that people were handed over to the United States by their fellow Afghans in settlement of some ancient grudge or ongoing quarrel? Was it possible to distinguish at any stage between Taliban soldiers who, as they understood it, were fighting for their people and nation and because the elders of their tribe had told them to do so, and genuine Al Qaeda terrorists? Some sort of fair trial is going to be necessary to sort that out. Yet the United States refuses to give them a fair trial. (A fair trial is the sort of trial that each one of us would like to have if we felt that we had been mistakenly arrested as members of a terrorist organisation.) If the Americans have got the right people, let them be tried in an international tribunal, or under American law. What have they got to lose? Finally all prisoners awaiting trial should be kept under humane conditions, whoever they are and whatever they are alleged to have done. The purpose of justice is not to seek revenge but to administer a fair penalty for proven offences. These men are not *proven* offenders, by definition, until they have stood trial. They have simply lost a battle. To repeat the question: why have we not protested about all this? Remember that many (moderate) Muslims see the actions of Western governments as a *Christian* response.

An attempt to take a balanced Christian view should not prevent us from taking a careful look at Islamic fundamentalism and even at terrorism when it has, at times, such a clear religious motivation. This is particularly important because these trends are part of our modern world and they seem unlikely to go away. Islamic fundamentalism, (and other religious fundamentalisms) as presently experienced, is hypermodern, a politics of identity. This identity is based on what Castells calls 'a double deconstruction'. The individual must give away (deconstruct) his or her personal identity and the nation-state must also lose its identity. Replacing these will be the *umma*, the ideal community (Castells 2004, 16).

Castells also puts forward an interesting description of the causes of Islamic fundamentalism. He sees it as a combination of successful state formation among some Muslim countries in the immediate post colonial period and also the failure of these same countries to cope with economic modernisation in the light of more recent technological innovation and global competition. A young, urban population has been left frustrated by this combination: they are well educated and relatively ambitious but trapped in 'no-win' economic situations. They have been joined by vast numbers fleeing the countryside. They are also aware that the state in which they invested so many hopes in the post colonial period is not performing; it is both corrupt and inefficient. It is also weak, particularly in terms of what they see as Western or worse still Israeli aggression (19). It is this situation which seems to have triggered off the 'Arab Spring', though the causes and outcomes of that vast and complicated movement are still unclear.

On the whole political Islamism has failed in its attempt to seize the institutions of the nation state (so far!). Organisations like Al Qaeda may be a last desperate throw resulting from the failure of more substantial projects. Whether radical Islamism has failed more widely in securing 'hearts and minds' remains to be seen. The jury is still out (22). The big issues in countries like Egypt, Tunisia, Morocco and Algeria may yet come down to the contest between Islamic fundamentalism on the one hand and secular modernity carried on the wings of a global economy on the other.

Strangely, fundamentalism is not really an attempt to renew ancient traditions but rather to take on modernity using its own methods. It is trying to turn religion into a rational method which can be used to combat others who have determined that their religion (or lack of religion) should be promoted by the same methods. In this sense fundamentalism is new. It has appeared for example in India (Hindu fundamentalism in this case) as a significant force only in the last twenty five years. Despite its supposed attachment to Hinduism its real model is the bureaucratic, nationalistic dogmas of Nazi Germany. Nazi Germany had an equally tenuous relationship with its myths. It was essentially 'modern' and Hindu fundamentalism is too.

And so is Al Qaeda. As John Gray says:

...Al Qaeda is ultra-modern. In organisation, it seems to be a hybrid of the semi-virtual business corporations that were so fashionable in the Nineties and the loosely linked cellular structures that run the world's drug cartels. Like the most advanced businesses, al-Qaeda is a worldwide network that is only vestigially territorial. Though some states may have sheltered it, it is not under the control of any

> of them. Thriving on weak government, and the mercurial mobility of stateless wealth, it is a perfect embodiment of globalisation.
>
> (Gray 2002, 50)

It may help us to think about the fact that terrorism has risen to such a prominent position in world affairs at the moment, not so much because it is an Islamic phenomenon but because it is a feature of globalisation. Terrorists are more than ever formidable today, not because they are sponsored by (Islamic) states, but because of the weakness of states which cannot control them.

> The crucial advantage possessed by terrorists today is that they operate in a time of globalisation and failed states.
>
> (Gray 2002, 52)

Arundhati Roy makes a similar point:

> Terrorism has no country. It's transnational, as global an enterprise as Coke or Pepsi or Nike. At the first sign of trouble terrorists can pull up stakes and move their 'factories' from country to country in search of a better deal. Just like the multinationals. (Roy 2002, 207)

This ability to move and change shape makes global terrorism a formidable enemy. It means that there is never one target. The United States, for example, which has proclaimed a war on terror, may feel that it has 'slain the dragon' (the Soviet Empire) but what it is now facing is 'a jungle full of poisonous snakes' (Rogers 2002, 58).

When even the world's most powerful state cannot subdue its enemies, an age of chaos and violence seems imminent. This is a nightmare which is as old as civilisation. People have always been terrified by chaos, and with some justice. Earliest creation myths had to do with the subduing of chaos by violence and the subsequent creation of 'the myth of redemptive violence' has permeated our understanding of civilisation ever since. In simple terms this means that we believe that we can only subdue evil by bringing a greater force to bear on it. This is of course a religion of fear, but then since when did we human beings really believe that love was the strongest power in the universe?

There is an instructive example of the fear of chaos in the Old Testament. It is probable that the tribal arrangements in Israel before the monarchy, a rather daring experiment in dispersed political power, may have foundered because of the belief that the nation would always remain impossibly weak if it did not have some centralised authority. The relative 'chaos' of the tribes could only be ordered by a king, and only then could the nation withstand the attacks of the Philistines. This led, it seems to me, to political tragedy. The move to monarchy was a step backward. Saul, with his back to the wall, is at least an understandable figure. The young David is attractive, but already the older man is showing signs of the corruption of power. Solomon demonstrates all too quickly what is wrong with monarchy as a concept. After that it is mostly downhill. It is only with the call and appointment of a servant that Israel's redemption begins to come closer again.

It is thus that the impact of terror on our societies strengthens our conviction that chaos is just around the corner and must be withstood at all costs. We have already mentioned Thomas Hobbes and his very human reaction to the chaos of his day. He described the life of man 'in the state of nature' i.e. without any recognised power to oversee affairs, as 'nasty, cheap, brutish and short', and his remedy was strong government. The individual must surrender his or her freedom to someone who had the power to exercise unquestioned rule. Tyranny, if that was the result, was better than chaos. Nor was this sort of thinking confined to Thomas Hobbes. The same fear of chaos informed the thought of many of the founding fathers of the Enlightenment. Descartes' rational method was, in one aspect, a control mechanism, a response to the chaos of the French civil wars and in particular the assassination of Henry IV which presaged a renewed bout of conflict after a brief respite (Brueggemann 1993, 3).

In a sense any sort of global order that we can devise is undermined by international terrorism. As we have seen, the nation state, on which we have traditionally relied for our security (Hobbes's solution) is deeply threatened today, not just by other nation states as in the past, but by the notion, and indeed the practice, of global terror networks. September 11, 2001 was so troubling because it was a premonition of chaos, and of chaos produced by an agent that might strike at any time and from any quarter. So it was that the United States declared war on terrorism and, apparently, gave itself permission to strike anywhere in the world in the name of that war. It is also the case that violence was legitimated and freedom sacrificed in the same cause. The United States and its allies have set themselves up as world policeman and gained a wide measure of support in that role because violence remains our only answer to violence, or so it seems.

How do we Christians respond to this new era of global insecurity and its reactive fundamentalisms? As Christians we may feel that we are uncomfortably 'on the fence', disapproving of the way that the West is creating painful spasms of cultural change, and yet quite certain that we want to have nothing to do with anything akin to violent reactions.

I have attempted in this section to deal with a number of issues to do with the way that we live in communities and the way we choose to govern ourselves—communalism, the idea behind the nation state, global government , the clash of civilisations including Christians versus Muslims, and world terrorism and its impact. I conclude, however, with a disturbing thought. Many of our Christian institutions are 'shell institutions' (Anthony Giddens' phrase). They look solid and robust but they are hollow. Why is this? In brief, the world has moved on and their structures are no longer applicable to the needs of the third millennium. We simply have not taken into account political, social and economic realities, as described in this section. If and when we do we shall find that we need new patterns for church and mission and new institutions to go with them.

THE CONTEXT OF FAITHFUL IMPROVISATION

Bible and theology

Discussions about context are directly relevant for those of us who take the Bible seriously, indeed it is from Biblical studies that we have derived the tag 'the critical hermeneutical principle is the context'. When it comes to the Bible and its interpretation it is easy to say what we do *not* want. We are familiar with the sort of use of the Bible which pays little attention to the declared meaning of the biblical authors and disregards the original context. A little of that is more than enough! What we *do* want, however, is more difficult to describe. How can we be sure we have got to the 'authorial intent' and how far do we follow the principle that the context is decisive in determining the meaning?

Let me give some examples of interpretation, all of them controversial in a minor way. In 1 Corinthians 11, the Apostle Paul is giving instructions to church members about appropriate behaviour when they meet as a congregation. He thinks it is important (verse 5) that women have their heads covered. Is this because there is some universal rule which is applicable to all times and cultures? Or is it that for a woman to have her head uncovered in public *in first century Corinth* was considered disreputable and offensive? If the latter, then the 'moral' of the story, so to speak, is that we should avoid acting disreputably, whatever that means in a given context. In the twenty first century a woman covering her head might still apply in, say, rural India; it would not in suburban Britain.

Another example, and a more contentious one, is the matter of women teaching in the church. There is a clear injunction in 1 Timothy 2:12 that they should not do so. Again, is this a rule for all time and all places? It may be so, but there are other possibilities. Timothy's church (probably in Ephesus) may have consisted largely of educated men and uneducated women—a common enough circumstance in the ancient world. This disqualified the women as *teachers*. They probably could not read and write let alone expound the Scriptures. Our context is obviously different. In a modern congregation there are plenty of educated women, some of them, perhaps, with degrees in theology! It is possible that the 'moral' of the text in question is that the teaching ministry should be in the hands of those who have the gift and qualifications to do so. For those, like myself, who were brought up in a denomination which depended on lay preachers, many of whom were encouraged to 'have a go' whether they were equipped to do so or not, this remains a significant point.

A third example: the ancient world projected the spiritual powers that influence our lives into the 'up there' and the physical environment, but this does not need to be the way that we do it today. What matters is that we understand that there are powers and that they are part of the life of institutions and structures. An illustration of this process might be that today there are indeed forces that create chaos and confusion—let us say certain aspects of the media—but we do not have to believe that there are chaos monsters in the sea, as the Hebrews perhaps thought. People make these thought transitions in real life without much difficulty. You do not meet even the most literalist Christians agonising about sailing in the Eastern Mediterranean because they are fearful that Leviathan will come and get them!

So here is my first point. We have to read the Bible in its context to make sure that we are applying it in the way that was originally intended. This is such a familiar idea that I do not need to take it any further.

My second point is less commonly made. In order to read the Bible faithfully we have to understand our own context as Bible readers, and that in two ways. Biblical studies can all too easily create its own world from which it is difficult to escape into the real world. We complain about biblical illiteracy, especially among the young, but biblical expertise is not much use if we never step outside our own boundaries. In the time of Jesus there was a sharp divide between the experts in the Law (that is, the *Torah*) and the ordinary people. Indeed the well-instructed like the Pharisees were all too ready to despise 'the mob' because they did not know the Law (John 7:49). In Matthew 23, Jesus was ready to describe the scribes and Pharisees as those who 'sit on Moses' seat' (v. 2) but he insisted that they needed to see that the burdens which they were imposing on others were intolerable (v. 4). We need to beware that our knowledge of 'holy things' does not betray us into acting in the same censorious and unloving way, preventing us from really entering into the struggles of people different from ourselves.

Secondly, we often forget that while the Biblical authors had their own *sitz im Leben* (life situation) so do we! All this talk about globalisation, postmodernism, postcolonialism and the like is necessary just because the terms incorporate not only world movements, but ways of looking at the world which go to make up our own particular worldview. If we really do have a postmodernist mind set for example—something we have 'picked up' from our schooling and our friends and the media—then that is something which we will bring with us to our reading of the Bible. This is not necessarily a bad thing: we all read the Bible with our own particular pair of cultural spectacles, but the important thing is that we are aware that this is happening.

Here is a very simple illustration. As we sit down to read the Bible do we start with a 'religion of fear' or with a 'religion of love'? In order to answer this question we need to have a measure of self-knowledge. What, for example, is my relationship to my earthly father? If I have had a fearful relationship with him then fear may be the key factor in all my relationships with 'authority figures', including God, and I may interpret messages from God accordingly. The reverse will be true if I have had a loving relationship. It is not a question of the authority or otherwise of Scripture. Love and fear may hear the same message, and accept it as true and relevant, but come to different conclusions. This sort of thing happens all the time. Consumer and producer may equally accept the validity of the 'just do it' slogan issued by Nike, but 'hear' very different messages all the same.

My third point is that contexts change. My own context changes all the time so that I am looking at the Bible differently today than I did yesterday. This should make us careful about coming to a full stop in our understanding of Scripture. As the Puritan John Robinson said, "For I am very confident that the Lord has yet more light and truth to break forth out of his holy word". It is also worth remembering that Biblical contexts change, indeed there can be a change of context even within the same book.

Take the case of Job, for example. There is a famous verse in the Book of Job where Job hears bad news about the loss of his possessions and family. 'The Lord gives', says Job, 'and the Lord takes away. Blessed be the name of the Lord.' (We often hear this quoted as an ideal response to hard times.) The text in question comes very early on in the story of Job (1:21) and events take a dramatic twist (again) almost immediately after he utters these words. In addition to all his other troubles, his health fails. The drama consists of the fact that instead of the trustful resignation that Job has shown up to now, he becomes depressed and angry. Also he protests his innocence. His illness, he says, is not the result of some wrongdoing, as his friends suggest. On this issue he is perfectly prepared to argue his case—with his friends and with God if necessary. The argument concludes when God says that Job is right (42:7). In the meantime Job has been brought to a position where he realises that he is ignorant of the full picture (42:3); he still has much to learn about God and his greatness.

The story as a whole suggests that there were several stages in Job's passion narrative, and that we can see human response to suffering as consisting of a series of responses or attitudes, each better and more mature than the previous one. At the bottom of the scale (not described in Job at all) are those who leave God out of the picture altogether. There is no God, or God is indifferent, and we humans will just have to get on with handling the situation as best we can. Stage two is represented by the attitude of Job's wife (2:9). 'Curse God and die' she suggests. 'Oh, yes, there's a God all right, and look how he treats us. I quit. I admit I'm embittered by life, but then that's God fault as well.' Job can recognise this attitude as wrong and can move on from there to stage three. 'Shall we receive good at God's hands and not receive the bad?' he says (2:10). This sounds very much like his initial response in chapter 1: 'The Lord gives and the Lord takes away. Blessed be the name of the Lord.' There is just one little area of doubt, however. It says that Job did not sin 'in what he said'. Is something else going on in Job's heart? Perhaps so. Be that as it may, with the arrival of his friends Job appears to be taking a very different line. He is anything but accepting. Instead he vigorously protests: 'I'm hurting, I'm depressed, God has "fenced me in", I wish I were dead'. Job's friends remonstrate with him, but he will have none of it.

My point is that this is stage four. Job is in a different—indeed, *better*—place than he was before. Resignation sounds trustful but contains all too easily an element of fear (which is the opposite of trust). In effect it says: 'I won't protest about this because I don't want to get into even deeper trouble.' Certainly I think that is where Job's friends are standing. They do not know God well enough, or they do not trust Him enough, to be able to conceive of anybody having an argument with Him. Those of us who have children are often disconcerted when our children 'answer back', particularly when they accuse us of being unfair. But we would rather that than their being so afraid of us that they 'agree' with everything we say, even when they really disagree in their hearts.

The theology of Job's friends is sound on the whole. We are all sinners; we reap what we sow; it is impossible for God to act unjustly—it all comes straight out of the textbook. But for all that, God says that they have not spoken correctly about him (42:7). It is Job who is right. God is much more interested in real relationships than in theological correctness. I think it is highly significant that when God himself finally enters the argument—to speak to Job—he insists that he and Job have a face to face debate and that Job 'braces himself and stands up like a man' (38:3 REB). 'No grovelling, please' says God. 'No keeping quiet for fear that you might lose the argument or get out of your depth.' I do think that Job has one more lesson to learn (and this is stage 5). He is not God. He does not have the whole picture. There are many monsters in the sea (41:1 ff) and Job cannot subdue them unaided. For these reasons alone he should not be surprised that life has some nasty moments.

There are five steps then, to be taken in ascending order:

- There is no God or, if there is, he is not interested in human affairs.

- There is a God, but I don't want to have anything to do with him because he means only harm.

- Life brings both good and evil. I accept both as coming from God but I will not question.

- I will tell God what I am thinking, even if what I am thinking apparently questions his purposes and his goodness.

- My 'debate' with God can be carried on with confidence but I should remember that I do not have the whole picture and God does.

Finally, let us go back to our verse: 'The Lord gives; the Lord takes away. Blessed be the name of the Lord'. Is Job here only part way through the learning process? Job may simply be saying the right or safe thing, being 'politically correct'. The overall context of the Book of Job suggests that this is so. In fact, Job may simply be wrong. (If he had got it right then no further test would have been needed.) The truth is that God gives, but he does not take away. The 'taking away'—which certainly happens in life, that is to say, bad things happen to good people—is a result of a fallen and sinful world. It is not, after all, God who brings calamity on Job but the Adversary.

Growing up—the process we see Job going through—means that we treat God more and more as a person. He is not an impersonal force but someone with whom we can argue. Equally, growing up helps us to de-personify evil. Evil things certainly happen, as I have said, but that is the sort of universe we live in. When God intervenes it is to bless us.

Let me give a simple example. If God gives a couple a child that is *meant* as a gift of love. He gives—blessed be the name of the Lord. If the child becomes sick and dies that is *not* God taking the child away. Nor do we have to 'bless' God for it. How we might respond to such a circumstance, however, is contained in the story of Job's 'growing up' in his relationship to God.

This is rather a long illustration perhaps to make a simple point, that even within a single book of Scripture the context may change dramatically. But it also illustrates the next point I wish to make: that on the whole contexts are complex and that they therefore need careful study. However much we dislike the idea, there is no substitute for a life-long endeavour to read the Bible carefully and to understand it thoroughly, if we are going to accept it as a faithful witness in our lives. Traditionalists (and I leave you to decide whether you are one or not) have got away with sloppy Biblical exegesis for far too long. In fact, they tend not to do Biblical exegesis at all, but to play a power game. This consists of marginalising their opponents because they are women, or liberals, or New Age, or overly-intellectual, or some such epithet.

My fourth point is that we need to be part of a circular process. Just as we examine our own context in order to read the Bible faithfully, so our reading of the Bible enables us to understand more fully what God is doing in the world which provides us with our context. In other words the Bible helps us to think theologically about globalisation, postmodernism postcolonialism and the other issues we have been discussing. This is something which we desperately need. Let me try out an example here. Supposing we think, as I do, that essentially globalisation is driven by market capitalism. Are there words to make this real to us as believers? We are reasonably comfortable with moral categories such as 'sin' and 'evil', but would like to leave politics and economics out of it, at least if we are talking about the kingdom of God. However, this is precisely the problem I am trying to address. We do not know how to handle political and economic discourse and, more seriously, we do not even realise that this sort of description is crucial to our reconnection with 'the time that now is'. Somehow we must connect theological description with other descriptions.

David Smith has some strong words about this:

> The nature of the relationship between the globalised, economistic culture and [the] message of Jesus Christ has become a central issue requiring urgent theological and missiological reflection (2003, 88).

and

> The deepest cause of the spiritual weakness of Western Christians when confronting globalisation is the nature of their relationship with the ideology which has driven this culture (2003, 89).

and

> Evangelicals have reacted to modernity with
> a strange mixture of intellectual defiance and
> practical accommodation (2003, 90).

Of course the well is not entirely empty. There are Christian thinkers who have been working to help us. Tim Gorringe, it seems to me, provides the 'urgent theological and missiological reflection' that Smith requires, in the following analysis (Gorringe 2000): (I am paraphrasing a lengthy argument.)

Sin is 'anything that makes the fullness of life impossible'. [Gorringe bases this on the saying of Jesus in John that he has come to bring fullness of life.] One of the effects of sin is alienation, from our bodies, from our work, from each other and from the natural world. In this case we can give 'sin' a name: it is the 'constellation of attitudes that makes possible savage capitalism' which 'takes away from us the world as home'.

If we begin to speak of 'attitudes' then capitalism becomes a spiritual problem. 'Sin' is the problem that sees the gap between rich and poor increasing all over the globe, that creates our ubiquitous shanty towns, that is alienating us from the planet. The answer to 'sin' is grace. Reality is seen, not as an opportunity for profit but as a gift to be shared. If we recognise the 'radical giftedness of life' we join the *ec-clesia* ('called out community'). We are not those who accept 'the reigning plausibility structures'. We do not say 'there are no alternatives', we look for ways of subverting 'the invisible hand'. In this we become ec-centric (Mark 10.43). Our centre is not the machine but the kingdom. This is not to be other worldly in the wrong sense. On the contrary, 'where sin makes us strangers, grace calls the world home'.

Capitalism is the fundamental problem because it will not accept limits, which is a spiritual problem. It is partly a compulsion to power, a drive for dominance. These perverse desires are what the Old Testament calls idolatry. The counter-education of desire there-fore becomes the task of the *ec-clesia*. Faith teaches us that this is not an impossible task (Hebrews 11.1). We need to believe 'in the power of the God of life to lead us on a new exodus away from the fish, cucumbers, melons, leeks and garlic (Numbers 11:5) of the global supermarket, to a homeland of vines and fig trees for all.'

Notice the way that Gorringe on the one hand refuses to give up the great theological words such as 'sin', 'grace' and 'faith', and on the other hand is at home in a particular economic (socialist) analysis. Whatever we say about the correctness of his theo-logical interpretation or his political analysis, it is without question that he is striving to bring the two together.

One word of warning here. Bringing politics and theology together does *not* mean the reintroduction of the sort of theocratic politics that typified many pre-modern societies. The Bible, an intensely political book, took a principled stand against 'theologising' politics in this way, right from the Old Testament onwards. Even Israel could not claim unqualified di-vine support. Rather, God promised to aid the nation if it kept the covenant and obeyed its laws. This has contemporary relevance. God is not 'on the side' of any nation. For example, if we are prepared to give the modern state of Israel some sort of Biblical sanction whatever its behaviour, then we have forgotten the provisional nature of God's dealings with nations. Furthermore, we shall never have a settlement in the Middle East, because there are plenty of Israel's opponents who make the same claim—God, they say, is on our side. As we all know, this is the point at which the argument ends and the fighting begins. I am not saying, of course, that we should not think biblically about the whole situation. In every human theatre God is concerned with issues of justice and human flourishing and with the spread of the Gospel.

I have ended this section at a rather controversial place. This is not a bad place to end. It reminds us that good Biblical interpretation is a hugely complex enterprise. Not an impossible one, of course, but one which will take a great deal of energy, thought and even courage.

History and tradition

There is something very powerful about our own history. It is important to us in all sorts of ways, filling our lives with unexpected meaning. Amit Chaudhuri in his introduction to a recent collection of Walter Benjamin's essays (Benjamin 2009) takes up Benjamin's own description of himself (as developed by Susan Sontag[23]) as someone who came into the world 'born under the sign of Saturn' endowed with slowness and hesitation, a sort of stubborn clumsiness.

23 See Sontag 2009, 107-34

Chaudhuri suggests that for Benjamin the 'sign of Saturn' was the shame of Jewishness, the sense he had that in some profound way he did not really belong, despite his intellectual prowess. That may be right. What is certain is that we are deeply affected by our history and by the traditions that we attach to our history. Even a rather simplistic treatment of the Jewish situation in twentieth century Europe like the drama *Fiddler on the Roof* captures something of the unease of Jewishness in the modern era: the balancing act needed to survive in a difficult world. So there must be at least two important questions here. What historical circumstances or 'secret histories' tug away at my life? They could be something very obvious or something which even I find it difficult to identify. But also, what can I do to confront them? We cannot change the past but we can change the way we deal with it.

Confrontation, however, is the difficult part, and some would say that there is a place for leaving well alone. Perhaps you can have 'too much history'. One thinks of all those stories in which families are reunited for some special occasion—a wedding, a funeral, an important anniversary—and all sorts of skeletons come tumbling out of the cupboard. I have recently read a novel, the plot of which hinges on the discovery by a widow of some letters which disclose that her husband had been unfaithful to her for many years, something which she had never suspected. One is not very far into the action before one feels that she would have been better off simply not knowing. 'Where ignorance is bliss 'tis folly to be wise' as the old proverb says.

Having said this, I suspect that the usual situation is rather different. Much more typically, important truths, when they are hidden or half hidden, are damaging us *because* they are not out in the open. I know them, but have not faced them. Or others know them and are acting accordingly, but have not 'let on'. Or, they are there somewhere in the atmosphere—a pervasive anti-semitism in 1930s Europe for example—but only materialise at moments of crisis. In almost all of these cases I suspect that the victims need firstly to find out as much as possible about what is going on, and then assess the personal consequences with a view to possible action.

Full disclosure seems to be part of healthy living and you see this again and again when people who have suffered some tragedy insist that they need to know all the facts. When others are at fault then there is usually talk of justice mixed with accountability and 'making sure this never happens again'. It is also significant that attempts to cover up a fault or misdemeanour are frequently thought to be worse crimes than the original event. Uncomfortably, all this often also sounds like revenge. There is, no doubt, a very difficult dividing line here. An outraged sense of justice is one thing; a wish to see others punished so I can feel better, is another.

From a Christian point of view where does forgiveness come into the picture? Over the past few years I have noticed that forgiveness as an ideal seems to have become less popular. It is treated sometimes as a moral cover-up. It is suggested that rather than 'having the matter out' we forgive people instead. The feeling is that they are then being allowed to 'get away with it'. This may be a misunderstanding of forgiveness but if the word has been devalued in popular use, then we are in difficulties. An unforgiving society— one that does not consider forgiveness necessary—quickly becomes an embittered and vengeful one. To put it another way, understanding is not just the business of getting the facts into the open. We have to forgive to understand. Until we learn to forgive we simply rule out the possibility of really grasping what is going on.

We do not have to put all this in the context of forgiving past wrongs. A better understanding of our own past may produce good news as well as bad. People researching their family history, for example, may be enlivened and encouraged by their discoveries, not just in the sense that they come across something of which they can be proud, but also something which helpfully explains a family mystery or illustrates a family characteristic. In any case, good or bad, the news seems to matter. There was a legend in our family that my great grandfather was a Yorkshire landowner who eloped with a Scottish heiress by the name of Lady Jane Gillespie. There seemed to be some substance in this because my father's second name was Gillespie. A little research, however, revealed a different story. Great grandfather—his name was John—was not a landowner but a butcher. Jane Gillespie did indeed feature in the story, only she was a seamstress, not an heiress. There was no elopement—the parish records tell us that they were married in their own local church, but the elopement part of the story may have stemmed from the fact that grandfather arrived one month after the wedding!

Now, I have to say that I greatly enjoyed investigating this story, not only the original but also the revised version. I felt I had got a little closer to my ancestors through it. It did not matter that in the course of the telling they had rather come down in the world. So long as they were real, and the history was accurate that was enough. Somehow there is something healing about putting a story straight or getting to the bottom of things, even when we are sharpening the knife that wounds us, or digging a hole for our prejudices. But, as I say, we want to know the truth of the matter. Finding out that the so-called facts are mostly guess-work, that the footnotes are not in place, so to speak, that my own prejudices have simply been replaced by somebody else's is very disillusioning.

Family is only part of the picture. The neighbourhood I live in, the place where I work, the church I worship at, all have their histories. We do well to be curious about them. Charles Powers' novel *In the Memory of the Forest* recounts how the Polish town of Jadowia is poisoned by the attempted suppression, after 1945, of the memories of what happened to its Jewish population. Most people in the town did not want to know that history, but it powerfully affected their lives all the same.

I live in a small end-terrace house in a newish housing estate—about twenty five years old now. It is a pleasant enough locality, quiet because there is no through road, near an extensive park with a couple of rugby fields; everything is surprisingly green and leafy. No one would pretend that it has much character, however. The houses are built to a predictable pattern, there are no sweeping vistas, no monuments, no architectural features of note. Some while ago I bought a map of the city going back to 1881. Of course the housing estate did not exist at that time. To my surprise, what did exist was a football stadium. (Did they have such stadia in 1881?) Furthermore the Texaco Garage which stands on the main road just where you turn onto the estate, is called the Stadium Service Station.

As I looked into it, I discovered more. The stadium was huge, holding potentially 30,000 people. Gloucester City Football Club, who occupied it for several years, had actually known great days with some outstanding players. The streets that now make up the Estate are named after them—(Stan) Myers Road, (Dicky) Coltman Place, (the goalkeeper, Ron) Etheridge Close and so on. You may be saying at this point: what does it matter? Who cares? Well, at very least it mattered to me! I felt quite differently about my neighbourhood once I found out that as I walked its streets I was accompanied by the ghosts of footballers past. But more seriously, why was the stadium and its adjoining land sold for houses? And what happened, as a result, to Gloucester Football Club? We know that it was relegated to an inferior site, a part of the town notoriously subject to flooding, but did this affect its performance? And what did it do to the morale of the City when the club was banished in this way?

I do not wish here simply to reproduce the argument (see above in 'Place') that we need to be rooted in communities in order to flourish. That is part of what I am saying, but I would also insist that we have to be proactive in discovering our history and keeping it alive, even when, perhaps especially when, it is painful to do so.

An important example of this process in this country is the ubiquity of war memorials. War memorials celebrate the courage and sacrifice of service men in past battles, but, as far as I am concerned, they have another, equally important, purpose. Whenever I stop and read the long list (it always seems inordinately long) of casualties relating to the 1914-18 war, I invariably feel a sense of angry incredulity. How could *that* have happened? How could we have been so criminally stupid as to lead a whole generation of young men to the slaughter? 'My subject is war,' as Wilfred Owen said, 'and the pity of war'. We can say a great deal about war, but that is the first thing we need to remember about it—that it is pitiful. If war memorials help us to remember that, they have done their job. I was on holiday in Derbyshire recently: a part of England full of interest. Strangely, the most memorable moment was standing in front of the war memorial in Buxton and finding the name of Captain Edward Brittain, M.C., Vera Brittain's beloved brother killed in action in 1918—you can read about it in *Testament of Youth*.

Christians, too, cannot afford to forget their history, again not in the sense that they need to read more Church history—though that would be a good idea—but because, like it or not, we are all 'the children' of some Christian movement or tradition handed down to us and shaping our Christian experience and worldview. So we Protestants are 'children of the Reformation'. In this country this accounts for the prejudice we have against Roman Catholics, by no means a thing of the past. (Equally, I suppose, Roman Catholics are children of the Counter-Reformation.) As an English Protestant I have to struggle against this prejudice on a regular basis. Words like 'Pope', 'Jesuits', 'Cardinal', 'Mass' simply trigger off historical associations beyond my immediate rational control, so that I have to call them up and put them in their place. Thus, if I think about it, 'Pope' can mean John XXIII as well as Pius IX; 'Jesuits' were the first missionaries to India in the modern era as well as the shock troops of the Counter Reformation; 'Cardinal' can be Cardinal Newman as well as Cardinal Richelieu; 'mass' is just another word for the Lord's Supper and so on.

Tradition is the history we live by—not much different from the idea of culture, the way we have ordered our lives 'to survive and thrive' in the light of accumulated experience. Modern people are very suspicious of tradition. You hear phrases such as 'the dead hand of tradition' and the adjective 'traditional' is often used in a pejorative sense. In practice, however, we cannot do without it. Language itself is a sort of tradition. So are the customs and practices that bind our society together. No doubt they need constant revision and adaptation; no doubt traditions can become tyrannical. But if and when we replace them, we need to find other traditions to take their place. Our church has traditions—small and great. In addition to the really important ones such as the sacraments or preaching the Word, there are less important ones. Somebody greets you at the door when you arrive. At communion the wine is distributed in small glasses (this is a Baptist church) but we all wait for each other and drink at the same time. We take up an offering, but visitors are invited not to contribute. These seem to me to be good traditions and I should be sorry to lose them.

I suppose the opposite of the word 'traditional' is 'radical'. I like the word 'radical'; it gives a strong sense of thoroughness, of doing the job properly, of thinking things through 'to the roots'. But it is also a dangerous word. It means digging up a plant with its roots, so that nothing remains. A plant that has been 'radicalised' will not grow again. There are no doubt some plants that need such treatment, but very often they need tending and nurturing and perhaps pruning rather than digging up.

A number of thinkers have warned us against radical political projects. In this connection, John Gray, drawing on the thought of the conservative political philosopher Michael Oakeshott, (Gray 2010, chapter 4) makes an interesting distinction between a 'civil association' and an 'enterprise association'. The former is purposeless, in a good sense; it aims at no particular project, its chief purpose is to keep the peace. The latter is actually constituted by its project or projects (p.81). Attention to tradition is then the primary mode of civil associations, because what holds a society together in their case is not a particular project but the community's willingness to submit itself to a common *torah* or *lex* as expressed in its traditions. I am reminded here of Gillian Rose's idea of the 'broken middle'. Rose believed that 'holding together' (refusing to be polarised) created the context from which the truth emerged. What was fatal was to allow project-type thinking to create divisions and factions. From the vantage point of these, the truth would always be skewed.

My main objection to this approach is that it does not sound to me like Jesus and the prophets. In a conflict where there is not much to choose between the two sides in terms of right and wrong—the First World War is an example—then it might be right to be situated in 'no man's land'. But are all contests like that? What if the struggle is between the strong and the weak, the rich and the poor, the bully and the victim?

Think, for example, of the way that some religious traditions have been formulated so as to exclude women. Is there not a case for some anti-patriarchal project? Nevertheless Gray and Rose (in their different ways) have presented a powerful case.

Think of those groups in which tradition has been jettisoned. The so-called house churches, for example, have sometimes scorned traditional ways and invented their own rules, only to find, in many cases, that they have handed themselves over to charismatic figures. The latent authoritarianism of these men (it is usually men!) could not then be held in check because there were no traditions or structures to which they had to conform.

The conflict between traditional and radical is often a titanic one. In the aforementioned *Fiddler on the Roof* the small Jewish community lives by its traditions, but they are daily being challenged. The milk-man Tevye has a number of daughters who push the boundaries of tradition in their own way. The eldest wants to marry the man of her, rather than her parents', choice. Another leaves home to join her revolutionary husband-to-be, already exiled to Siberia. Yet another wishes to marry a Gentile. Here Tevye feels that he can no longer disregard the tradition. His arguments for and against—'on the one hand' and 'on the other hand'—come to an end. In this case, he says, 'there is no other hand'. Tevye knows that a community which ceases to live by its rules soon ceases to be a community.

Saving our traditions is similar to defending our places. We are not sure whether we ought to be defending the past or not. On the one hand we laugh a little patronisingly about people who are always talking about 'the good old days' and on the other hand we are not at all sure what it is of our 'inheritance' that we can afford to give away. We want to be open to change but are also aware that change is not always a good thing. We are increasingly alienated from the past but know in our bones that it is a country, a context, that we need to visit regularly.

The context of other faiths

There follows a very brief account of a very complex and well-rehearsed topic, but my concern here is the simple fact that religion is not something we can ignore when our overall theme is contextualisation. Religion is inextricably part of culture and 'culture' is an umbrella word for context, at least in the sense that we tend to use the word 'culture' nowadays. The secularist idea—popular fifty years ago—that religion is on the way out as education undermines credulity, carries less and less weight today. Whether we think that religion is a good or bad influence, there is little evidence that people are abandoning it.

It would be easier from a Christian point of view to explain the world without the presence of the other world religions. In a general account of revelation—what we believe God has revealed about himself to humans—how do we account for multiple ancient systems of belief? We Christians cannot pretend that we are alone in representing theism—far from it.

One simple approach might be to suggest that all religions are roughly in the same relation to Christianity as Old Testament Jewish faith was to the New Testament church. In brief, a sort of fulfilment pattern. World religions are a *preparation* for the Gospel. This was a very popular approach at one stage amongst Christian theologians, perhaps less so today. An example would be the way that a group of Christian students of Hinduism developed the idea of a faith journey beginning in Hinduism (rather than Judaism) and ending with an acknowledgement of the uniqueness of Christ[24]. A natural implication of this approach is that there are true believers in every religion; their faith saves them and their ignorance excuses them. (Think of the character Emeth in C. S. Lewis's *The Last Battle*.) Jesus is the universal saviour ('God was in Christ reconciling the world to himself') whether they know that or not. They are like the men and women in the Old Testament who never knew about the incarnation and crucifixion, but whose faith was 'counted as righteousness'.

24 A useful summary of this approach can be found in Boyd 1969.

Of course this is not to deny that religion can be the problem rather than the solution. If it is merely a man-made attempt to 'establish our own righteousness' (as the Apostle Paul might have put it) it may actually be a hindrance because it opposes God's grace. (This is more or less Karl Barth's approach.) On these grounds, Christianity, as a religion, is as much the problem as any other religion.

So, once again, we Christians need to think it through. At the moment it may be that we are rather confused. We realise that 'fundamentalism' is a term that secularists are applying to religions of all varieties, and most of us Christians would rather not be tarred with that brush. However, allying ourselves with moderate co-religionists also raises some difficult issues to do with the uniqueness of Christ and the nature of Christian witness. The borderline between religion and culture is a further difficulty in the whole debate about contextualisation. Can you be loyal to Christ and remain within a Muslim or Hindu or Buddhist culture? Phrases such as 'dual belonging' and 'insider movements' are becoming increasingly popular. In theory these issues of contextualisation are no different from attempts to make the Gospel relevant in a global or postmodern context, except that there is a long and troubled history of inter-religious conflict. This is also our context in the sense that it is part of our history.

THE CONTEXT OF PERSONAL GROWTH

Understanding ourselves

What strikes me very often about people is that there may be a gap between what they are saying about themselves and what I actually think they believe. I am not talking here about deliberate attempts to deceive, but about the way we build a persona which comes between us and the world. I think we all do this, but where it is a consistent self deception, it leads to weaknesses and ultimately disintegration.

Somebody came to see me the other day because he was finding it difficult to believe in God. We talked about that for a while, but it seemed to me that he really wanted to talk about something else, or at least the cause of his doubts was not what he said it was. Despite the fact that nowadays the debate about whether there is a God or not is quite widespread—ever since Dawkins and Hitchens and the like got going—he admitted that he had not done any reading on the topic one way or another. When he rehearsed his doubts, and I played them back to him, so to speak—they were the traditional ones such as 'God of the gaps', God as a crutch, God as wish-fulfilment and so on—he had to hand a perfectly adequate response to all of these issues, in fact in some ways he was more eloquent about them than I was. What seemed more significant than his intellectual doubts was a clear disillusionment with Christians and their behaviour. He found church very difficult; he only went because he thought his son enjoyed it, but it was not doing anything for him, and there was no sign of what you might call Christian fellowship. He did not seem angry with God—something you come across a good deal when things have gone wrong in people's lives—but he did seem disengaged, even bored with God. He was very much into extreme sports and relished a mental and physical challenge, but he could not see that being a disciple of Jesus might also present a challenge. (I suggested that if he decided to accept that challenge he might find God more real. Somebody he knew in the action rather than in the theory.) Much of our talk was also about relationship and trust, which was interesting again because I thought that there were relational problems in his life, but he was not able to express them.

Now the purpose of this story is to illustrate that at several levels my friend seemed unaware of his true motives. In fact I suspect he had little self understanding. The doubts that had come into his mind were generated quite simply by the fact that Christianity was not working for him. It was rather like someone who has spent a lot of money on an important piece of equipment and then finds that he is not getting any value out of it. He then draws the conclusion that the equipment is not worth having in the sense that it is a dud, it will not work for anyone. Mind you, I think that much of our theology is like that. There is nothing wrong with it, it is perfectly sound, but it is not being used; people are not getting the good of it. I run a little discussion group at church, called

Hard Questions, and my judgement is that most of the people taking part are heretics. This sounds bad but it is not. They consistently express views that are not really mainstream Christian views at all, but they are their views, and we trust each other enough to be able to express what we actually think about things. There is not a significant gap between what they say they believe and what they do believe, and perhaps even more importantly they are trying to make their beliefs work for themselves. This is much more healthy than saying what they think they ought to say and even more healthy than people who say what they believe but, without knowing it themselves, actually believe something else.

To return to my friend, the gap between his protestations and the actualities of his life were expressed in a number of ways. As I mentioned, he is very much into extreme sports and he attempts a number of these, often very unsuccessfully because he is overweight. There are in fact good physical reasons why he is not achieving very highly. However, he is unable to be realistic about his chances and indeed about the factors that are spoiling his chances. He knows that he is overweight and he speaks very dramatically about the way that he is going to lose weight in a short space of time. But this is also unrealistic. He relies on unaided will-power and this does not really work. We are all inclined to dream impossible dreams, and that may not be a bad thing, but in this case, repeated failures at the grand attempt are likely to lead to terminal discouragement. What is even more interesting is that he does not see this. He reinforces his unrealistic expectations in terms of achievement with unrealistic descriptions of his abilities, strength and will-power.

What does this mean? Always the most difficult context which I inhabit is myself. It is certainly the most difficult to know. Also, if there is a gap between what I think about myself and reality, then that gap is likely to be filled. If belief in God is not working for me then I will find something else that I hope will work. Then I will find reasons for not believing what I believed in the first place.

I want to draw an analogy here. I recently read a book called *The Spirit Level* (Wilkinson & Pickett 2010) that suggests that the primary cause for the ills of society is inequality. It is not, as you might think, poverty itself that is the problem, rather it is where you have rich and poor living near to each other and the gap between them is evident and painful. The book demonstrates this in a number of ways, referring to almost all the important indices of a happy and healthy society. Now, in the same way, though we attribute our difficulties to other external causes, it is often the gap in our self understanding that is the real problem. We may not understand very much, we may not have much information, but the important thing is that our thinking, and therefore ultimately our behaviour as well, should be based in a solid way on that information—we should not be fooling ourselves. It is quite possible for somebody who is information rich also to be fooling themselves, to be unable to understand themselves well enough to interpret the information they receive, however good it is. In fact, as we have implied, it is the gap which does the damage. Thus one could add to the famous saying 'mankind cannot bear too much reality' the equally true saying that 'mankind cannot bear too much unreality either'.

My friend is not a happy man and he is not an effective man. He is putting a huge amount of effort into fooling himself. He was not, I think, trying to fool me when he described his dilemmas. He was not in that sense trying to put on a front. He was not trying to impress me, or not usually, in our conversation. He was much more trying to impress himself. He was being open and sincere with me as far as I could tell, but I also think he was not being open and sincere with himself.

Is there a remedy for all this? Yes, I think there is. It has to do with what I was saying about the discussion group. We cannot close the gap between my faulty self-understanding and who I really am without the help of other people. Honest friends in a trusting relationship are obviously the best solution. It is not really a matter of friends who can give me advice, but the creation of a sort of pool into which I can drop the pebbles of my thought and see what the ripples are; it is a 'forum' in which I can hear my own voice and observe what effect that voice has on the people I am with. What worried me most about my friend was not that he was having doubts about God but that he did not seem to have many Christian friends.

To summarise: we understand ourselves best in context, in the company of those who know us best. It is appropriate, therefore, that our next section is on relationships.

Relationships

It would be quite easy, many of us feel, to grow impatient with the numerous sermons we hear condemning 'individualism'. Family, friendship, (see immediately above!) community, relationship are extolled almost *ad nauseam*. It is not by chance, therefore, that the more we have the means to do so the more we arrange our lives so that they are not dependent on others. The wealthier we are the more detached our dwellings, cars are 'sexier' than public transport as well as more convenient, the Internet is such a hit not just because it puts us in touch with people, but because it allows us to relate to them on our own terms. The extended family is not really that popular in the wealthy West and neighbours are often more of a trial than a blessing, especially if they are noisy.

And yet...

While most of the above is true for most of us, there is a strong sense in which we would want to affirm an opposite set of propositions. None of us wants to be considered friendless or unneighbourly. We spend much time trying to make families work—especially when they don't work very well. We are fond of grand-children perhaps, or find it rewarding to dig into our ancestry. Pubs and clubs and churches continue to flourish, simply because they bring us into contact with others. Some Christians are currently making a renewed attempt 'to live in community' despite a history of failed experiments in the quite recent past. They are doing this because they are quite sure that there is something better than our current isolated living arrangements.

So what is an appropriate context for Christian living in the light of this debate? I have to say that the communitarians win hands down. Both in terms of our ethical duty and ultimate wellbeing (and when we think about it those should amount to the same thing in the long run) there is a very strong case for saying that the desirable and healthy context for human living is other people. 'It is not good' (in all sorts of ways) 'for people to live alone'.

We may all be nodding at this point but it is a challenging conclusion. If it is true that without a context of meaningful relationships we are alienated from our real selves then we have to take seriously the following propositions.

Churches are not primarily 'places of worship' but opportunities for relationship. Our current preference for church attendance over church membership (with an option to move if we are dissatisfied) by no means meets the criterion for effective Christian commitment. The New Testament reference to being parts of a body teaches that there is, or should be, something organic about membership and that leaving the body is like amputation!

Long-term, faithful, relationships are very important to God, whatever their character. Any move on our part to make such relationships difficult, or to create division where there is unity, is not what God wants. Relationships come in all shapes and sizes and as long as there is a mutuality about them and they are not abusive or coercive then they are to be encouraged. We would do well as Christians to look at the issue of gay and lesbian relationships in this way. In truth, all sorts of relational arrangements can be viewed thus.

Heaven, as described in the Book of Revelation in the Bible, seems to be convivial. We do not have to make too much of this, as we do not really know what the next life will be like, but, speaking generally, there does seem to be an emphasis on crowds, cities, communal events and the like.

George MacDonald said once that 'we cannot get nearer to God by getting further away from people'. Of course we think that we can, and put a very high value on times of quiet, retreats and so on. We also feel that we have Dominical example, which is reassuring. However, I suspect it depends on our motives. The right use of solitude is not a means to avoid people but an antidote to the superficiality of being too busy.

Practical sharing, including our money and time, lies as much behind the New Testament idea of fellowship (*koinonia*) as feelings of warmth and friendship.

Wealth separates us from people. 'How hard it is for a rich person to enter the Kingdom of God.'

Tasks such as learning someone else's language and culture are at the heart of having effective contextualised relationships with people who are different from us. This is hard work.

We live in a society which is contra-community and which therefore makes good relationships difficult. We are often complicit in this. We have to learn to be counter-cultural and yet to be accepting of the fact that our context is our context. If we were to list some of the contra-community aspects of our everyday lives—detached housing, car travel, supermarkets, the internet, the nuclear family and so on, and then said that we had to give them all up in order to be disciples, I think we would be moving in a non-contextual direction, emulating the sort of life-styles favoured by, say, the Amish in Pennsylvania or some orthodox Jewish groups. Now these groups may have a great deal to offer—they are certainly hugely supportive of their members—but they are much stronger on identity than relevance. Contextualisation is not their strong suit. Somewhere, somehow, I feel we need to be both contextualised and counter-cultural and this is a complex task. To put it in rather simplistic terms, with regard to our culture we need to be both prophetic and affirmative. Remember Jeremiah whose task was 'to uproot and pull down, to destroy and to demolish' but also 'to build and to plant' (Jeremiah 1:10 REB).

Cars can be used to give people lifts; homes to offer hospitality; the Internet can keep me in touch with people I might otherwise have lost contact with; the nuclear family means I can give my children the attention they deserve. But beware! We so often think that we are using possessions and arrangements to serve others and to live more fully human lives, but instead they are using us. Our lifestyle is turning us into selfish, dysfunctional people, operating well enough when the sun is shining, but isolated from our nurturing and supportive context, and too distant from our neighbours to know how to love them.

Career choices and guidance

In addition to the challenge of self-understanding and making the most of relationships, for most of us there is the important context of our career or job. This has become increasingly problematic. Having a career, or if that is too grand a word, a life-time job, was much more common not so long ago. Now, for many people, that sort of marker may be missing. They have skills rather than jobs, move about looking for the best opportunities, are not offered long-term employment, may have more than one part-time job, and re-train frequently, trying to build up a portfolio. Does this matter? Perhaps not. There is certainly no stigma attached. Someone I know who runs an employment agency says that he is positively suspicious of people who have been in the same job for a number of years. Have they got stuck? Do they lack ambition? Nevertheless there is some loss here, some erosion of identity, and we are very short of identity affirmers in our society today. Place used to be important in this respect, but our increasing mobility has changed that. The fractured family certainly does not help. We have fewer institutional loyalties. Postmodern people are more isolated, live more fragmented lives.

How does our identity as working people relate to our lives as Christians? Here I think we get entangled with some rather difficult questions about priorities and guidance. How do we decide what God wants us to do with our lives? As an illustration we could consider the conversion of Saul of Tarsus which we read about in Acts 9. Saul, whom I shall now call Paul, is, when we first meet him, a man who has a very clear life work—briefly described as maintaining by all means a strict Judaism. As we know, it is in the pursuit of this work that he is 'on the Damascus road' but there he is confronted by a set of circumstances that changes his life's direction entirely and in the end gives him a new identity. So drastic was this change that later he asserts that those crucial components which once made up his previous identity he now considers worthless (Philippians 3:4-8). His new work starts almost immediately upon conversion and becomes so important to him that it overrides all considerations of cultural identity and personal convenience (1 Corinthians 9:19-23).

It is possible that we might feel a little jealous of Paul. His certainty is highly attractive! However, I am going to claim that Paul too lived by the rule that 'the critical hermeneutical principle is the context'. What persuaded Paul to take on a new direction in life? Well, we may conjecture that Stephen's death had something to do with it (Acts 8:1). What is certain is that on the Damascus Road he saw a light and heard a voice, that he was blind for a while and that a man called Ananias helped him to understand what was going on (Acts 9:1-19). These were events, circumstances, that he could not afford to ignore. They were the new context in which he must now interpret the whole meaning of his life. You will say that God intervened in his circumstances to bring this about. I would say that God usually acts in this way. It is not true that we can only confidently say that God is at work when he intervenes in a spectacular way in which human agency is largely absent. For one thing even spectacular guidance or deliverance is a 'circumstance' which we can ignore or reject. As

Paul said to King Agrippa, 'I was not disobedient to the heavenly vision' (Acts 26:19), but presumably he could have been. Also Paul is perfectly happy with a much 'lower' version of circumstantial guidance. He decides not to go to Corinth because it will be too painful for everyone (2 Corinthians 2:1) and decides to leave Troas because Titus is not there and his mind 'could not rest' (2 Corinthians 2:12,13). The truth is that God *usually* guides us through our circumstances. Not that God overrides my choices by moulding me through circumstances as if there were some sort of machine at work which stamped out uniform shapes. Context is not God, but God is in the context.

In the Development discourse there is a saying 'the Jericho Road sets the agenda'. This means that I cannot afford to by-pass or neglect an urgent need, particularly if it is a matter of life and death. But it may have a wider application. Why should the Jericho Road not always set the agenda? What is wrong with the idea that what we ought to do in any given situation is what God wants us to do, defined by love for Him and love for our neighbour? There are some satiations, no doubt, in which there does not seem to be any right or wrong; it is a matter of pure choice. Also there are situations when we do not know the rights and wrongs of the matter. But most of our contexts provide us with clear moral choices. Is it ever right that, confronted by such a situation, God asks us to break His rules?

The tough Biblical example here is Abraham's 'sacrifice' of Isaac. On the surface this looks as if it is a clear example of God asking somebody to do what, by normal human standards, would be considered to be wrong. This is an incident over which Biblical exegetes, ethicists and philosophers have argued a great deal. My own belief is that Abraham was wrong in thinking that Yahweh wanted him to sacrifice his son, and that Yahweh saved him from his own decision by providing a substitute. It is nevertheless commendable on Abraham's part—in fact an indication of his faith in God—that he went ahead on what he believed (wrongly) was God's wish, even though this would have been at huge cost to himself. In the same way Jephthah was wrong to sacrifice his daughter and wrong to think that Yahweh would require him to keep his vow in this way.

Both these incidents are examples of people being prepared to do something that they would normally consider to be wrong—killing their own children—because God had ordered them to do so. This is by no means simply a dilemma we find in the pages of the Bible. There are plenty of Christians, for example, who neglect their families—something which cannot be right in itself—because they believe that God has given them a 'higher call'. The verse usually employed to back this up is Luke 14:26. It is true of course that we have to put God's call, that is to say our Christian discipleship, before our family, if there is a choice to be made. That is the plain meaning of the text. But if this entails doing something wrong, then, I submit, it is not God's call.

What I think a verse like Luke 14:26 is talking about is the danger of making my family an idol, so that it becomes a sort of 'my family right or wrong' situation. If my family loyalties, for example, make me unjust in my dealings with my neighbours, then

I must learn to put justice before loyalty, because, as God's servant, justice always comes first. A simple illustration would be something I came across recently. A man was interviewed (on the radio) and asked to comment about the practice of putting a false address on a child's application form so that the child might get access to a better school. He said that potentially he would be prepared to do this because 'it was for the sake of the family'. This was so even though he realised that somebody else's family would miss out.

When Jesus resisted the appeals of his family to withdraw from his ministry (as appears to be the case from Mark 3:21) he was not on any evidence *neglecting* his family. Indeed we have an example later of him taking special care to provide for his mother, even *in extremis* (John 19:26,27). The context of family is in this respect the same as every other context. There are responsibilities and pressures. We have the opportunity to do what is right and what is wrong. We cannot lay aside the constant struggle to know what this means and to put it into practice, on the grounds that God wants me to love Him and serve Him. Loving God and loving my neighbour (which includes my family!) are indivisible. Is not this the logic of the incident which ends with Jesus telling the parable of the Good Samaritan (which is where this discussion began)? Jesus tells the lawyer that the way to life is love of God and love of neighbour. The lawyer asks for a definition of 'neighbour' and Jesus tells a story which shows that 'neighbour' is the person God sends to us. The Samaritan who loves his neighbour—the mugged traveller—shows by his loving action that he also loves God. The Priest and the Levite try to divide the two. They think that they can love God (Jesus deliberately chooses men in God's service) without loving their neighbour. To put it more widely, we love and serve God primarily by acting in a loving way within the context that God has given us. Using God as an attempt to lever ourselves out of that context is at best mistaken, and at worst hypocritical. In Matthew 15 (see verses 3-9) Jesus does not accept that the scribes and Pharisees had the right to neglect their parents because the money which would have gone to support their parents' old age has been 'given to God'.

Not that I am suggesting that the choices we have to make are always that easy. The trouble with families is that they are part of our identity. Serving God is usually, we feel, to do with some other sort of identity. The fact that families are a 'given' is compounded by the fact that this is a 'life-sentence'. Most people have responsibilities to family at every stage in their lives. This very often clashes with our chosen life work, especially so if we believe that our work is what we do in a special way to respond to God's call. This clash of identities, so to speak, is common enough, and can seldom be avoided. What we do need to avoid is pretending that God has absented himself from either side of the equation. Whatever the context, he is there, and requires that we should honour him.

THE CONTEXT OF CHRISTIAN MINISTRY

A good place to begin when we think about Christian ministry is the church, both local and worldwide. Most Christians are involved in churches and, despite some disillusionment with the institutional church, on the whole Christians accept that church is a necessary context if they are to thrive in their Christian lives and be active in Christian ministry.

The Church's Identity

What sort of an identity should the church (local and universal) have? Manuel Castells can help us here in distinguishing three sorts of identities—*legitimising*, *resistance* and *project* (Castells, 2004). He applies this taxonomy in the first instance to people but it works equally well for institutions, including churches.

Legitimising identity is the role the Church is given as part of civil society. The police or the law courts would have a similar sort of identity. On the whole it is a positive identity because society needs, or believes that it needs, these sorts of institutions if it is going to 'survive and thrive'. It is this standing—something that society subscribes to because it is something that it thinks it *needs*—that brings legitimation. In other words the Church may have a legitimising identity if society believes that it stands for something that affirms and strengthens it. Perhaps it is seen as the guardian of society's morals, or as its conscience. It did not have this role before Constantine, but it did once Christianity had become the state religion. Christians vary in the value they put on this identity. Established churches rate it highly; groups like the Anabaptists are more likely to feel that it is a curse rather than a blessing. In any case most church people feel that the good opinion of society at large is worth having as long as this does not subject the church to undue pressure to conform.

Resistance identity is produced by reacting to these pressures to conform or more seriously to systems of domination, as when the Church is undergoing persecution. Typically this produces 'non-conformist' churches, communes and communities, house churches, underground churches and the like. These marginalised and persecuted communities take on a new identity by virtue of the very fact that they are resisting pressure to conform. They stand against the values of the dominant society and deliberately reinforce the boundary lines between them and the community. The Church has often had a very marked resistance identity. It is typical of the apocalyptic literature in the New Testament for example. Even where the Church is not undergoing persecution as such, it may have a resistance identity derived from its sense that the dominant ideology is undermining its effectiveness and even its existence.

Project identity is a building of identity out of existing resources with a view to change. This produces 'subjects' in the sociological sense, people who create new meanings as against those prescribed for them by the existing society. A church may assume a project identity if a) it is not simply expressing a legitimising identity or b) not acting in accordance with a resistance identity, but rather *acting upon* society to bring about change. The foundation of the primitive church in the context of mission (e.g. Acts 1:8) suggests that it had such an identity.

We can relate the three identities above to the distinctions made in H. Richard Niebuhr's *Christ and Culture* (1951). The first (legitimising) would come under Niebuhr's heading 'The Christ of culture' whereby there is no great tension between church and world. Christians can be at home in culture. The higher and deeper Christians' understanding of culture, the better they will see that Christ is there. The second (resistance) goes to the other end of the spectrum—Niebuhr's 'Christ against culture'—where there is a sharp division between the values (and therefore the behaviour) of Christian people and 'the world', or culture as it is customarily experienced. The third (project) lies somewhere in between, perhaps best described by the category 'Christ the transformer of culture'. This suggests that we can be affirmative about culture because it is God's creation. However, being human it is part of the fallen creation and must be restored through Christ and his people.

My thesis is that we are badly in need of churches which have 'project identities'.

Churches are new communities, and not just another product of society—a Neighbourhood Watch scheme, or a tennis club—nor are they sects, with limited entrance and closed exits, proclaiming their defiance by means of their difference. No, they are *projects*, and it is what they are trying to build—the Kingdom of God—which gives them their character.

Church Growth

As a result of the Church's project or missiological identity there is widespread agreement that churches should be growing. Church people are convinced that we should expect church growth, or to put it another way, growth is a sign of a healthy church.

This, however, raises other questions. What is growth for? What sort of growth are we experiencing? Are we investing in the right sort of growth? The simple equation 'bigger is not necessarily better' comes immediately to mind. There has been a good deal of talk in recent times, some of it rather triumphalistic, about the growth of the church in the non-Western world, particularly in sub-Saharan Africa, Latin America and also in parts of Asia. This is often placed in the scales against the way that the church is shrinking numerically in Western Europe and perhaps also in the United States. Andrew Walls, by no means a triumphalist, has chronicled the way that the centre of gravity in world Christianity has begun to shift decisively away from the old centres that have dominated Christianity to new ones previously thought to be non-Christian (Walls 2002, Part 1). I am not sure that I hear quite the same optimistic note (with the exception of some from the Korean church) when I speak to thoughtful Christians from the non-Western world. I think this should make us pause. Let me list what, as I understand it, disturbs them and then comment a little further.

One way of explaining the current situation (a 'history of religions' approach) might be that global Christianity is currently being contextualised into primal religion; 'animism strikes back', so to speak. Where the West has offered an over rationalised, powerless and unholistic version of the faith, those who are more in touch with 'spirituality' through their local traditions have rediscovered a more vibrant and effective Gospel. Evidence from Africa in particular is that the fastest growing churches are those that rely heavily on 'signs and wonders', particularly healing ministries. Emotion and enthusiasm play a great part in their worship. Charismatic power is recognised and put to work.

But is this the whole picture? There are also many who are advocating the rejection of *traditional* ways in favour of some radical fresh start. Young people, especially young men, are taking the lead, and there is a heady mixture of independence, excitement and 'prosperity thinking'. These new arrangements, subject as they are to considerable global influence, seem to promise freedom from the old colonialist past as enshrined in the 'mainline' Christian churches (Roman Catholic, Anglican, Church of Scotland and so on) which look back to the age of the dominant missionary society. This is now a familiar response but what is new is that they are also inclined to reject the authority of the 'independent' churches and its re-emphasis on the indigenous principle. For the newest wave of enthusiasts, this linking with the indigenous past seems little more than an exercise in syncretism; also it keeps in place authority structures, such as the rule of elders, that they are hoping to escape.

This rejection of authority in an ecclesiastical setting sometimes spills over into rejection in other spheres as well. In a study by Rik Van Dijk which refers specifically to Malawi, the then President, Dr Banda, was attempting to use traditional cultural practices to bolster the waning political authority of his ruling party. The rejection of traditional practices by the leaders of the new young churches then became a means of asserting political as well as religious independence (Van Dijk 1998).

Is this rejection a good thing or a threat or just a natural and innocent development? The most worrying aspect, I suggest, is the rejection of the past, in terms of a new religious or spiritual rootlessness. I have already given my reasons why I think this is dangerous in a general sense, but for the Church it is particularly so. The religion of experience isolated from Scripture, from the handed down tradition of the church and from the witness of human reason, is hopelessly adrift. It quickly falls into the hands of charlatans, demagogues, and exploiters, particularly those with charismatic personalities and authoritarian mind sets. Also, and this is my main point, it is prey to some of the most worrying aspects of globalisation. I am thinking here of the lure of Western 'prosperity'.

We have to face the fact (welcomed by some) that the Western global life-style is deeply attractive to many people who see themselves, temporarily they hope, excluded from it. The image of the 'illegal immigrant' attempting by all means possible to cross the barriers into the 'promised land' of a more affluent society, may serve as an image of millions of the world's population who see the global culture as something they would gladly enter if they had the means.

Of course when they do manage to get to this particular 'promised land' it is often immensely disappointing, but that is a truth they usually discover too late. An amusing illustration titled *D-Day*[25] shows the 'invasion' of a remote island (Caribbean or Pacific perhaps) by Disney forces. The troops are clones of the Disney character Goofy and they are under the command of Donald Duck and Mickey Mouse. Disney has some allies. The flag they are planting on some high point has the Microsoft logo. Offshore a battleship, proudly bearing the Nike swoosh on its prow, fires tins of Coke and flies the McDonald's flag. The landing craft have the insignias of major oil companies on them and a Motorola aircraft drops televisions.

To my mind there is one thing wrong with the picture. The locals are fleeing in terror from the invaders. I doubt this as a portrayal of the reality. I suggest that in practice they are welcomed with open arms! It is ironic that the official emblem of the Society for the Propagation of the Gospel shows a similar, if more ancient, scene, with a British warship just off the coast of a remote island. A clergyman in full clerical dress is standing on the prow and holding out a Bible. The 'natives' are rushing down to the shore eager to receive what the ship is bringing. The banner draped over the scene bears the words (in Latin) *'Come over and help us'*. The irony is of course, that the Gospel was not, unlike the products of the Disney invasion, all that welcome.

25 See *New Internationalist*, December 1998.

What sort of growth are we talking about, then? Much of the Christianity on offer, it seems to me, is a sort of 'prosperity Gospel' (usually with origins in the United States) that has more to do with 'prosperity' than 'Gospel'. Globalisation strikes again. Whereas the patient and difficult transmission from a Westernised Gospel to an indigenised Gospel was effectively being made, over a period of time, this process has been subverted by a populist American Pentecostalism which offers not only the blessings of Christianity but a much desired link with the supposed good things of modernity.

This is particularly attractive to young people but not just young people. Brigit Meyer begins her account of Pentecostalism in Ghana by describing the experience of a woman in her eighties who has recently joined a Pentecostal church and who, as a result, is refusing to go along with traditional practices. This refusal, according to Meyer, echoes a sentiment often heard among Pentecostals summed up in the phrase, 'Make a complete break with the past'. Meyer's main point is that Pentecostals believe that they have got hold of a 'global' version of Christianity much superior to the local traditions from which they have broken away (Meyer 1998).

Chapter 2 of Richard Werbner's book *Postcolonial Subjectivities in Africa* (2002) is a moving account of a Kenyan young man in Mombassa who expresses his extreme alienation from traditional society by means of models taken from the Afro-American urban rap and hip hop counter culture. 'By choosing Afro-American culture as their example they differentiated themselves from their parents' generation and opposed the old colonial hegemony.' In fact they were protesting against the ideas of local African ethnicity and traditions which in Kenya also meant resistance to the state. ' They marked a radical rupture by deciding to define themselves as modern and 'American' (52-4).

Of course there are those who welcome this development. They see it as young people having the right to express their own cultural preferences, and finding the Gospel already to hand appropriately inculturated. Perhaps, but what are they losing as a result? What about the culture of their parents and family? What about the longer tradition of Christian faith that 'classical Christianity' represents? These are admittedly the 'old ways' but are the new ways better? A 'global' worldview will always answer 'yes' to that question, because it worships the great god Progress and whatever that worship means it certainly forbids you to look back to the past.

The dangers of a triumphalistic and 'prosperity' approach are easily translated into the experience of the local church wherever that church is worldwide. It has the same characteristics everywhere—an emphasis on numbers, a desire for the spectacular, ecstatic worship, the offer of the good life if certain conditions are fulfilled, a tense relation with tradition and the past, and quite often a tendency towards apocalypticism. The context that nurtures this sort of church is a consumerist, economistic, spectacle-rich, celebrity worshipping , excitement-at-all-costs, rootless, global culture, such as the Domination System serves up regularly through its media outlets.

Christian education

The complexity and variety of the various contexts that we encounter today indicate that we need a more thoughtful and thoroughgoing approach to education of our own Christian people. This could be in a church or in a wider setting such as a Bible or theological college. Perhaps the main issue is that so much of our instruction is irrelevant to the real world. Often we have a good message but we seem to be speaking into a vacuum. My advice to preachers, for example, is to spend as much preparation time on studying their congregation as on the content of their sermons. Learners, too, often find that they are in the curious situation that they can see what the issues are but they do not seem to matter. They do not answer the 'so what?' question.

The task of understanding our context however difficult cannot be avoided if we are going to be effective teachers. To put it another way: if our messages are not contextualised then they will not work. In this area too 'the critical hermeneutical principle is the context'. David Lundy is very good on this. He is writing about leadership but virtually everything he says can apply to training. (Lundy 2002, chapter 9.) He points out that every year Procter & Gamble conducts 1.5 million telephone calls surveying its customers and potential customers! How much time and effort do we spend finding out about the background, capabilities and needs of those we are teaching and training? Here are some of Lundy's points:

- Christ's incarnation is the supreme model of contextual ministry.

• Contexts are hugely complex. We must not seek to simplify that which defies simplicity. In the same way, cultures are often *mixed* cultures with no one tradition able to claim that it is 'essential'.

• There is no substitute for hard work. We must read, listen, visit, observe. People's cultures can only be learnt by spending time with them.

• The teacher needs to take the initiative in building a cultural bridge to the learner (not vice versa).

• There are two cultures to be learnt: the one you are working in and the one you are working with. Or you might say three: Biblical, organisational, target.

• Working from theory to practice there is almost always a necessary process of simplification going on.

This last point deserves an illustration, because differences in culture are often a question of differences in scale. If you travel by train in India it is advisable to take notes of the smaller denominations and some small change. When the time comes to buy your (essential) coffee and bananas it is no use offering the vendor a Rs 500 note. He knows what the note is worth and you are offering a perfectly valid currency but the scale is too big for him. He cannot offer you the correct change. So it is that the currency of our communication must often be broken down into smaller portions if it is to suit the context.

Good teaching also depends on effective community. Zygmunt Bauman, in a recent book worrying about our loss of true community, pins down our communication difficulties to the prevalence of 'individualism' helpfully described as 'the denial of collective, public vehicles of transcendence and the abandonment of the individual to the task of discovering meaning which most individuals lack the resources to perform alone' (2001, 6).) He speaks of the *agora* and *ecclesia* (14)—the public space and the called out gathering—and suggests that the balance has tilted in an unhelpful way towards *ecclesia*, because of the strong drive in our society to individualism and the 'colonising' of the public sphere by this process.

In terms of education, the task is to reconnect individualised people with public knowledge. In part this is by discovering 'that there are more ways of telling a story than are dreamt of in our daily storytelling' (13). It also means to widen the possibilities of choice by systematically reviewing those aspects of our public life that we have relegated to the realm of 'no choice' (13). (The frequently heard comment that our economic situation allows for 'no alternative' comes immediately to mind.)

In more practical terms, we need our Christian education to be informed by the discourse of the modern social sciences: sociology and culture studies, first and foremost, but also politics, economics and development studies. This creates a discourse which uses Scripture and the teaching of a wise science. Social science of this sort helps us to see the world in a more complex way and to attack the natural fatalism which constantly disempowers us. For example, churches hoping to connect with their urban environment should be guided by the insights of a good up-to-date urban sociology.

This all sounds rather daunting because there is so much out there that is relevant. Some sort of selection will be necessary and some ability to put what we select into an educational framework. What, to begin with, are the issues that the people we teach really feel that we should be addressing—issues that capture their imagination and impel them into the action? Is it green issues, fair trade, debt remission, unfair labour practices, medical ethics, freedom issues (injustice, torture, warfare, arms trade, refugees etc.)? I am sure there are many more. What is the relation of our Christian education to these issues? Are they the same issues that we might choose if left to ourselves? In other words, is there a gap between educators and learners when it comes to areas of vital interest?

Another approach would be to try and *look at the context missiologically*. I conducted a survey recently which asked a selection of mission leaders and thinkers what they thought the big, or at least the coming, issues in mission were. They responded with a long list[26]. This selection is of interest in itself but anyone involved in Christian education might profit by the thought that the church is first and foremost constituted by the mission of God (*missio dei*) and the more we put our teaching and training into the context of mission the more we give a right perspective on the Church's role in being a sign of the Kingdom.

26 Published in the mission ezine *Encounters*. See 'Emerging Themes in Mission: A Survey and Summary' www.redcliffe.org/encounters Issue 26 October 2008

The teaching and training rooted in the contextual approach which I have tried to describe is much more demanding than the traditional educational model. It moves us decisively away from the authoritarian mode of education, in which we are the sole source, and invites a more dialogic or empathetic style. It undermines our certainties, and educationally this may be a good thing. When we teach we have to realise that we have people with different constructions of reality. 'It's all in the mind', we say. Well, educationally speaking, where else would it be? It is much more difficult therefore to take a 'one size fits all' approach. We need to hear the 'little stories'. Observing the context of those we are training and teaching reminds us of its *variety*. Metanarratives in terms of people's culture are clumsy instruments. Take the way that we in the West refer to Africans or Asians. Are all Africans alike? Of course not. Must we distinguish the complex cultural histories of Asian people? Yes, we must.

I am reminded here of a mission team sent out from this country led by a Westerner but including two Asians, one Japanese and one Korean. Their assignment was in Phnom Pen and the team leader paired up the two Asians on the grounds that being both Asians they ought to get along well. The two of them were standing in front of the pile of skulls in the museum erected to commemorate Year Zero. The Korean said to the Japanese. 'That's the sort of thing your people did to my people'. So much for Asian harmony!

It is not all one way. People coming from the premodern, typically those from the Global South, are often confused by the cultural history of the West. They think that re-presenting the pre-modern worldview will be a suitable way to challenge the modern. But what they are confronting is the postmodern, something they have never met before.

However our 'contextual' teaching happens, and whatever frameworks we use, people need to understand the dynamics of 'the world we're in' . Whether we describe it as reading 'the signs of the times' or hearing 'what the Spirit is saying to the churches', to use another Biblical phrase, or simply insisting that trends in society, like any other trends, must be heeded, this is a vital aspect of our education.

N.T. Wright says in his book *Jesus and the Victory of God* that Jesus gave a clear message to the people of his day that they were rushing headlong to destruction, and they ignored it (Wright 1996, 383). Perhaps we are in the same situation. In fact I find a good deal of 'sales resistance' to this idea among Christians. Mostly it is disguised as a 'super-spiritual' contention that the *agora* is none of our business. We are in any case far too busy with the *ecclesia*. I am reminded here of what the philosopher Gillian Rose says:

> No one and no community is exempt from the paradoxes of empowerment. (Rose 1996,5)

The truth is that far from spending too much time on the 'city and its laws' and 'the paradoxes of empowerment' we are, even in a book like this, not really 'grasping the nettle'. The trouble with looking at the future in terms of movements and ideologies, useful as that might be, and then trying to construct a suitable outline for Christian education that will help us adjust to this new situation, is that, as an approach, it is too *functionalist*. We are in a life and death struggle and the purpose of mission is not to accommodate to the world but to withstand it. Simply analysing trends phenomenologically and then adjusting our missionary techniques to it will not do. Education of this sort will not equip our people for the battle ahead. Further, the battle will only be won if we have a renewed vision of the Kingdom of God. The mission of the church has always been essentially to do with God's purpose to establish his kingdom and through that purpose to bless 'the kingdoms (nations, peoples) of this world'. It was so when God promised to bless all peoples through Abraham's descendants and it is so today for us who are Abraham's descendants. This purpose has always been opposed by the evil Empire. We remain in a Mustard Seed versus McWorld situation. We study missio dei to know what God is doing in the world. We study the way of the world so that we can recognise the enemy.

Some final questions about education:

• To what extent are we finding out what *experience* of God those we are instructing actually have? Can we start from there? That experience is also part of the context.

• What is the future for which these people think they are being prepared?

• Are some new methods and styles of instruction required: stories, Freirian approaches to problem solving, mentoring, apprenticeship models?

• Is there space in our teaching for listening to voices from 'outside'?

• Do the learners really know how to *apply* their theology to themselves, to their specific tasks, and to building the Kingdom of God? In this sense, are we sufficiently learner centred?

• Is our teaching and learning sufficiently integrated? Are we asking people to make the connections for themselves—if they are there!?

• Is our style of teaching sufficiently interactive? Are we preaching, designing study programmes, organising the teaching environment, group sizes etc. with this in mind?

Witness, dialogue and translation

Outside of the church fellowship, in our approach to people who do not know the Gospel and are unchurched, we normally use such terms as 'witness' or 'outreach'. There are two other words, however, that possibly have more contextual appropriateness today, namely 'dialogue' and 'translation'. These may fit better because in practice we are in a day-today situation in which we are forced to be more circumspect about our communication of the Gospel.

Let me explain. The idea of dialogue has always been controversial for people who believe that they have a message to proclaim. The term presupposes, at the very least, that I am in the presence (context) of somebody who is different from me, with whom I might agree, but could as well disagree. It is not far off from the word 'debate' which assumes an opposition, a more adversarial context. This in turn can shade into the idea that I am encountering an enemy (a 'duel' is taking place, perhaps) and the language of 'attack' and 'defence' becomes appropriate. This uncertainty about the role of the 'other'—fellow explorer, verbal sparring partner, harsh critic, implacable enemy—creates a number of dilemmas. Let me list some of them.

• Speaking very generally, if we withdraw from the world ('separation') we can lose our ability to communicate. If we merge with the world then we lose our distinctiveness and are not sufficiently different to have a message or impact. (See the 'island' illustration above.)

• In the process of dialogue are we aiming to confront or are we seeking consensus? Jesus and the prophets were frequently confrontational. On the other hand, consider Aesop's fable.

> The wind and the sun had a contest to see who could get a man's coat off him. The wind blew for all it was worth, hoping to tear the coat from the man's back. However, the more he blew the more the man wrapped his coat closely about him. 'Let me try' said the sun and he shone on the man with all his warmth. Before long the man took his coat off.

In my experience a 'reasonable' approach, even in the face of unreasonable power, often achieves better results than confrontation (but see the next bullet point).

• People who are trying not to be confrontational are often accused of 'sitting on the fence'. This is clearly a term of disapproval, so we might like to look for another one. 'Living in no man's land' might work, though the clear implication is that this is a dangerous place to be, because you can get fired at from both directions. The philosopher Gillian Rose, as already mentioned, favoured the term 'the broken middle'. Andrew Shanks describes it in this way:

> Rose's philosophy springs from a fundamental refusal to think in terms of 'an innocent us against guilty them', the mentality of group belligerence. Rather, it is a prophetic project of bringing to light the very deepest conflicts by which one's culture is fractured, in order to mediate between the opposing parties, so to speak, as a referee. (Shanks 32-3)

Or again:

> The 'middle' is the place where our wanting to be recognised as innocent is necessarily 'broken', just because here we are exposed to everyone's judgement, and our claims to be innocent will never satisfy everyone. (34)

There are gentler terms, such as 'holding the ring' and perhaps we ought to cultivate these because the language of dialogue is always being upstaged by the language of combat.

• In practical terms, the most intriguing approach to dialogue that I know of has been provided by Walter Wink in his description of what he calls 'non-violent engagement'. (Wink 1992, chapter 9) This is a sort of dialogue, but of an assertive nature, midway between 'fight' and 'flight' as Wink himself puts it. The idea is to face up to unjust and oppressive situations by refusing either to back down or to respond violently, but by seizing the moral and psychological initiative. The oppressor would be confronted by his own injustice and left uncertain as to how to proceed, while the victim, now no longer a victim, emerges as vindicated, however much he or she suffers. Of course this is a 'dialogue' for a context of oppression. A dialogue between equals would be different.

• Perhaps the deeper issue is: who can we do business with? At the heart of this question is a theological debate about whether the Powers which have fallen are redeemable. (Wink 1992 chapter 4)[27] Can we dialogue with a *system*, as in 'the Domination System'? In any epic which stresses good and evil, light and darkness, the only real option is struggle. In J. R. R. Tolkien's *The Lord of the Rings* there are few if any characters (Boromir may be an exception) who are partly good and partly bad. They are either wholeheartedly on one side or the other throughout, or, if they change sides (Saruman, for example) then they are lost to the other side permanently. In the Lord of the Rings you do not dialogue with Sauron, or even an orc. This is an important

27 See also the brief comment on this material in Howard-Brook and Gwyther (2002) p. 265 with footnote 78.

debate because in practical terms it poses such questions as: should Christians work within, say, the arms industry to redeem it, or should we have nothing to do with it? Some would say that there is Scriptural warrant for both. Revelation 18:4 commands Christian believers to leave the world Empire, Babylon, before they get caught up in its destruction. On the other hand Jesus himself speaks of his disciples as being 'in the world, but not of it' (John 17:15). The difficulty of discerning the rights and wrongs of the matter is reflected in the way that the debate over these verses and others like them has never been resolved.

• A considerable band of thinkers (Carl Gustav Jung is the most famous) believe that evil is essentially the 'shadow' of good and that there is the possibility of integrating the shadow back into the substance, perhaps even to the extent that no shadow remains at all. This is obviously in sharp contrast to the dualistic worldview just described in which good and evil are constantly at war with each other, a war which can only be resolved by the complete defeat and eradication of one of the contestants. Expressed in a different sort of picture, evil is a contamination or infiltration of the good world and in that way co-inhabits it, but will finally be removed by some purification process—the most typical biblical picture is a refiner's fire.

• As I have already suggested, how we envisage others may materially affect the way we deal with them, down to such important issues as where we decide to work, how we do our shopping, who we invite to speak in our churches and at our conferences, where we invest our money, where we send our children to school, and so on. It will also affect something as important as how we *feel* about life itself. In a way the 'context' here is in my own mind. I remember visiting a Hindu temple in Southall in West London some years ago with a group of students: a sort of Religious Studies field trip. A friend who lived in Southall had helped to organise the visit, and he remarked to me that as soon as he entered the temple he was aware of some sort of evil presence. I did not know how to respond to this. I had spent much of my working life in India and was, by contrast, experiencing a bout of rather pleasant nostalgia (it was the smells that did it) and could not detect any evil however hard I tried! Now the point of this story is not to say who was right and who was wrong but to suggest that the context, and here I mean the worldview that each of us brought with us, probably determined the sort of experiences that we had.

My second preferred term when describing the church's witness is 'translation'. There are two main things about a good translation. The first is simply that it has to be faithful to its original; the second that it must be intelligible to its users. You will probably remember when you were at school the moment when you looked at a slab of inscrutable French or German prose and however much you puzzled over it you could not make head or tail of it. The problem in communication here was a fundamental one. If I did not understand the original I could not explain it to others. In the same way, if I have not understood the Gospel for myself I cannot impart it to others.

Yet in translation work there is a second equally important principle. The translation has to be understood by those for whom it is intended. However well I understand the original I have to communicate this understanding in terms which are familiar to my audience.

Much of our preaching in the local church fails at precisely this point. What we say is true enough. In one sense it is faithful Gospel preaching. But it is not 'heard'.

Why is this so? There may be many minor reasons. We may be using technical, in this case theological, language which is familiar to us and not to others. Or, after a fashion, we may know the original too well. Perhaps we have such an easy familiarity with the Gospel that we cannot express it in an idiom which is different from the one to which we are accustomed. And this is near to the chief point which I want to make. The main reason why we find it so difficult to translate the Gospel is precisely because we have made an idol of our own culture. We have to smash that idol and set ourselves free to express the Gospel in a culture which is alien to us if we are ever going to communicate cross culturally. Immersing ourselves in somebody else's culture and beginning to see the world through their eyes is such a difficult thing that it is very seldom attempted, let alone achieved. Yet it is the only way to achieve full translational intelligibility.

I think we can all see the force of this argument when it comes to the person working in a foreign country with a different culture. Yet it applies equally to situations in this country. There are many middle-class churches which are simply unable to communicate the Gospel in a working-class environment. They insist that converts or potential converts become middle-class and 'respectable' in their outlook and attitudes if they are to join the church. This is a form of cultural imperialism and confuses my cultural preferences with the Gospel itself. If the church is predominantly middle-class and in a predominantly middle-class area, then some sort of cultural adaptation on the part of those from other cultures may be reasonable.

More frequently we find middle-class churches which are located in working-class areas, creating cultural ghettoes for themselves, and then wondering why nobody comes into the church. There is much talk of mission no doubt, but very little willingness to reach across cultural barriers, which is the very essence of mission.

Mission

Wider even than the term 'witness' is the term I have just used—'mission'. Anything which is being done under the call and direction of God and which involves a move into unfamiliar circumstances might be called 'mission'. The root of the word is the verb 'to send' so it is not possible to be a missionary, 'a sent one', if we stay at home, or, as we say nowadays, remain in our comfort zone. By definition mission involves an encounter with a new context, and, as usual, understanding the context is crucial. The old insistence that missionaries be 'long-term' and learn, as a priority, the language and culture of their new location, is not an outmoded idea. In this area too 'the critical hermeneutical principle is the context'.

Nor is this simply a matter of better communication. God works differently in different cultures. Kirk Franklin of Wycliffe International testifies that during a period of spiritual renewal in Papua New Guinea he was able to enter in a profound way into what was going on, while his wife was not. This was not because he was more 'spiritual'. While they were both Australian nationals, Kirk, unlike his wife, had been brought up in PNG and was much more familiar with the culture.

Without wanting in any way to limit the power of God, it seems to be the case that mission works best when it is finds a trigger or triggers within the local culture. This is because we are all humans, and none of us operates apart from our culture. Lesslie Newbigin writes powerfully about this when he explains 'the logic of election'. God does not (normally) communicate with us 'through the skylight', but rather through our neighbour and more widely through our circumstances. We are not designed to be independent monads, but to be fully human only within a network of (human) relationships. Mission has to accept this reality. The people we encounter are a bundle of memories, ideas, emotions, responses and desires, all of which are culturally conditioned.

My own belief is that we do not spend enough time discerning other people's cultural preferences. On an individual basis we might do well to ask someone the simple question: 'what makes your heart sing?' (and conversely 'what makes your heart sink?'). At a wider level what is it that people are doing by choice, what are they watching, who are they pleased to see, what do they want for their families, what do they sacrifice time and money for? I realise that this may seem rather human-centred, as if we need only to find out people's preferences and they will tumble into the kingdom of God. Surely, we might say, the claims of God's kingdom are often quite contrary to human desires. Jesus introduced his offer of the kingdom with a call to repentance, a much more demanding approach than asking people what makes their heart sing!

And yet there may not be a contradiction here. John the Baptist preached repentance too, and a much fiercer version of it than Jesus did. We read in Luke's Gospel however that huge crowds came to hear him and that (in one translation) 'people's hopes began to rise'. John, and in due course, Jesus too, were popular because however demanding their message there was a promise of radical change. The context was one of hope and despair. There was much hope that change was coming but there was also that sickening feeling ('hope deferred makes the heart sick') that they had been told this story before. (It was the opposite of today's situation where we are surrounded by novelties, but do not really want to change.) So Jesus in his inaugural sermon at Nazareth announces the Jubilee and explicitly assures the congregation that the time of fulfilment has come. My point here is that Jesus was aware of the desires and expectations of the people and was ready to respond to them. Though he had a tough message, it was not an irrelevant one. Quite the reverse. It was carefully matched to the political, economic and social *needs* of the people who were listening to him. About how many sermons today can the same be said?

It would I think be possible to pick through the history of mission and find a number of 'triggers' that were important for the spread of the Gospel. This would be a useful thing to do, no doubt. But, if my theory is correct, most of those triggers would be context specific. For example, the church in Korea may have grown rapidly because becoming a Christian was, at one stage in Korean history, almost a patriotic duty. But you could hardly expect the same mixture of history and patriotism in the UK today. Better than trying to plunder history would be the careful study of our own culture. Missiology, I would contend, is not just learning about St Paul's missionary methods, or William Carey's missionary principles, but about the world we are in.

Let me try an experiment. David Harvey, a geographer, suggests that we can draw up a systematic account of any given society by means of the following analysis (Harvey 1996, 78-9).

- *Discourse* – how we describe things, language, symbols, representation

- *Power* – who is boss, 'who shall serve and who shall eat'

- *Beliefs, values* – how the world is, how it can be better understood, how I can be in it

- *Social relations* – the various ways people relate to each other

- *Institutions, rituals* – the organisation of our political and social relationships e.g. the law, education system

- *Material practices* – our material environment and our relationship with it e.g. urban or agrarian landscape

The church of which I am currently a member is on a slightly down-market housing estate in a well-known English city. The estate is fairly well defined geographically, so that it is possible to make generalisations about it, as one might about, say, a village. I do not know the estate all that well, but using the grid above I can begin to describe it. The accuracy of the analysis is not the question here. I am trying to illustrate a technique. Here are some of the preliminary notes.

- *Discourse/language* Obviously the main language in use is English, but not a very complex or literary English. (Preachers will need to bear this in mind.) Many of the other means of representation are visual. Music is also important, but it is not the music of the church.

- *Power* Power is mostly exercised through the family. It is absolutely necessary to understand social relations to make sense of the way that people are free or not free to make decisions.

- *Beliefs* Formal beliefs are not clearly articulated. Many are what might be reasonably characterised as superstitious. Values are derived from the traditional sources—family, school, peer group, the media, but often lack structural support.

• *Social relations* See 'Power' above. As in all societies these are complex. Family is crucial, but because many families are dysfunctional, people need (and sometimes get) a wider range of social relations through clubs, social services, churches, neighbours, friends.

• *Institutions/rituals* These are in short supply. Schools are important, as is the rugby club. Churches are not very prominent in the estate's life nor are shops, post offices, local government offices and the like.

• *Material practices* Generally rather depressing. Much of the housing is tawdry and even dilapidated and there is scarcely a beautiful building in sight.

Now, these are the merest beginnings of an outline. I am not even sure that they are fair or accurate. I am only trying to illustrate a useful technique for those doing mission on the estate in question. Indeed I would go further and say that careful attention to the context is *always* required if we are to do mission well.

Miracles and the 'supernatural'

Many Christians feel that the direction of supernatural power—healing, exorcisms, extraordinary Divine communication—is an important part of Christian ministry. These ministries, too, need to be seen in context. On the subject of healing, for example, it might be good to begin with some words from Leslie Weatherhead.

> Health is correspondence with environment.
> If man *[sic]* is, as most would agree, body,
> mind and spirit, then the health of the spirit
> is its correspondence with its environment,
> and the name of that environment is God.
> (Weatherhead 1934, 26)

We have a tendency to be double-minded about the subject of healing and I am not sure that this is always a bad thing. I overheard a conversation the other day between somebody who had a painful tooth abscess and a sympathetic listener. The sufferer was explaining that the pain had started on Friday evening, and being the weekend she had found it difficult to see the dentist. She was therefore going to ask for prayer for healing (it was now Sunday morning) until she could get an appointment with the dentist, probably on Monday. This did not strike her, or anybody else to my knowledge, as incongruous, though it did catch my attention.

For most of us Christians our attitude to healing—here meaning Divine healing or miraculous healing—is at the middle point on a scale or spectrum, a position we have reached because we do not feel comfortable at either end. Thus, we are not secularists or unbelievers and would not take the attitude that the best (and only) remedy is to find what medical help we can, and that is the end of it. On the other hand, we do not despise medical help or believe that praying for healing by a miracle rules out going to see the doctor or having an operation.

So what? Well, as I have said, most of us are in the middle, somewhere between these two options. We think it appropriate to pray for direct Divine intervention at times and to get medical help at others. What makes the difference, I would suggest, is not the quality of our faith—you will hear this taught from time to time—but rather the context. We pray, and act, differently depending on such varying circumstances as:

- The medical help actually available

- The nature of the illness

- Factors such as age and future prospects

- The need for a statement of faith or a witness to God's power

- The mental condition of the patient

- What we believe God is telling us about the situation

Let me elaborate a little on these.

If there is no medical help available, as would often be the case in New Testament times, or the medical help is inadequate, then it would seem appropriate to ask for Divine intervention. Conversely, if there is help available then we feel we should go ahead and use it because that is also God's provision. There is a famous (and rather silly) story which illustrates this point. A man is trapped on the top storey of a burning building. A fireman using a loudhailer shouts a message: 'go down one storey, there's a fire escape you can use', but the man shouts back: 'no, no, I'm waiting for God to rescue me.' A ladder shoots up from below offering another way of escape, but the man refuses it. 'I've prayed that God will save me' he says. A helicopter hovers overhead and a winch descends. Again, the main refuses to act. Finally, the man is engulfed in the flames. Talking the matter over later with God the man is aggrieved. 'I prayed for a miracle and you did nothing' he complained. 'Really', said God. 'I sent you a message, and when that didn't work a ladder and then a helicopter. What more did you want?'

Certain illnesses, perhaps, only respond to prayer, or to be more exact, prayer reveals the causes of the illness which are not physical. (Counselling may reach the same point.) In James's letter (5:13-16) it would seem to me that the prayer and anointing by the elders is to be distinguished from short-term crisis healing needs. If someone has been injured in a car crash, get them to Emergency as quickly as possible. If they have become chronically depressed because of their disabilities (perhaps sustained in the same car crash) then get the elders to pray for them.

To whom does 'the prayer of faith' mentioned in verse 15 belong? My guess is that it belongs to the sufferer. Chronic illnesses classically need a change of attitude on the part of the sufferer. Notice that the passage specifically mentions the need to confess sin and equally the need that people have to know that their sins are forgiven (15,16). I was part of an eldership which used to pray and anoint regularly. We felt we had to be careful to avoid any sort of 'magical' approach, and as part of this we began by asking people something about their circumstances, and whether they felt the need to sort anything out before we prayed. In some ways this became the most important part of the process. One lady, suffering from a chronic illness, came to us, but asked that the team that anointed her should not include the pastor! Dealing with that broken relationship cleared up the medical complaint.

While Divine healing does not need to be seen as part of what we sometimes call 'spiritual warfare', exorcism does. I am unhappy, however, about the way that spiritual warfare has been confined in some circles to demonology. I think it is a misappropriation of the Biblical material. One approach that works well in the modern context is to see demonology as descriptive of a power struggle. It also helps if we can concentrate on the demonic (adjective) rather than the Devil or devils (nouns). Clearly some sort of 'spiritual warfare' is described in the Bible (see e.g. Ephesians 6:12), and we probably do not take this sufficiently seriously. However the source of the evil that confronts us is ultimately human wickedness. It was human rebellion that caused the fall and it is human sin that feeds into the 'lake' of evil which in turn is the source of the structures of domination which Paul mentions in Ephesians. G.B. Caird, commenting on the 'abyss' in Revelation 9:1ff, puts it like this:

> The abyss beneath symbolised all that had so far escaped the control of the divine sovereignty, a reservoir of evil from which human wickedness received constant reinforcing supplies. This does not mean that they [writers of apocalyptic] put the blame for moral evil on impersonal forces beyond the determining and responsibility of man. The infernal reservoir was fed from the

> springs of human vice. It was the collective
> bad conscience of the race, from which
> came the haunting and avenging furies.
> (Caird 1966,119)

Individual humans, even those with good intentions, are unable to 'wrestle' with these powers without God's help. ('You know how', says Paul, 'in the days when you were still pagan, you were carried away by dumb idols.' 1 Corinthians 12:2)

It is probably not helpful or necessary to believe in a personal devil in the sense that there is an independent centre of thought and will in the universe other than God and humans. (A statement of belief in a personal devil is not included by the Church Fathers in any of the great creeds.) The issue of personality seems to me a complicated one whenever we are speaking of something which is not strictly human. God is personal of course, but He is more than personal. To say that God is a person is the truth, but not the whole truth.

Satan, however, is less than personal. We can speak by analogy as if he has a personality but, I submit, we do not really mean that he is an alternative centre of conscious will. Thus the Bible speaks of him as an Accuser or Adversary and we know very well that often, for very human reasons, because we are depressed or have low self-esteem, or something of the sort, that we hear a 'voice' which accuses us (compare the experience of Jesus in the Wilderness). There is usually no harm in our personifying this voice ('Satan said to me') but that is just the way we use language. When John in the Book of Revelation wanted to use dramatic, pictorial language to describe the new confidence that the work of Jesus had achieved for us, he said that 'the great dragon was thrown down' (Revelation 12:9 cf. John 12:31) but he did not mean anything different from Paul when Paul says 'there is now no condemnation for those who are in Christ Jesus' (Romans 8:1).

When I say 'there is usually no harm' I ought to say that often there is indeed harm done by 'personifying' the idea of the devil, and we should be careful about it, even as a form of speech. Firstly to set up an alternative source of authority in the universe which is a personified evil in contrast to God who is personified good is a dangerous dualism, which leads to the sort of nonsense put about by Frank Peretti and co., and which portrays life as some sort of cosmic struggle between the Light and the Dark. This is indeed a heresy, and quite an old one, called Manichaeism.

Secondly, our spurious demonology distracts us from the real battle, the struggle against the evil structures—ideologies, fashions, corporations, false gods—which control our world. Thirdly, there are serious pastoral considerations. You cannot redeem Satan. So, by extension, someone who is in Satan's grip cannot be healed, only delivered. So my depressed friend does not need help for his depression but deliverance from the Enemy. But this absolves me from the perhaps long and difficult task of finding out what human factors lie behind his or her depression and what might be changed in his or her psychological, social or even physical circumstances that might make a difference.

The weakest part of this whole argument has to do with the unabashed way that the Gospels speak about demons (with a small 'd') as if they had a will of their own. But even here, I wonder whether we have read the stories of exorcism sufficiently carefully. Behind each of them there seems to be some human factor—fear of scribal authority, epilepsy, lack of self-esteem, trauma as a result of Roman brutality, and so on—which challenges us to see that something is going on at a deeper level. Too often we have read the exorcism stories in such a way that we cannot find a way of using them today. We do need a ministry of exorcism and I go along with Bill Wylie Kellerman when he says:

> We stand in need of what the Gospel calls 'exorcism'; liturgies [statements of the truth about God] which engage the powers at the level of their mythic and spiritual claims on humans and human cultures.
> (Kellerman 1991, 102)

THE CONTEXT OF INJUSTICE

I suspect that most of us Christians, at least here in the West, approach injustice issues with a degree of uncertainty and even guilt. Too often we are part of the problem rather than the solution. Many years ago I was in the audience when the late Professor Bruce was asked the question: which group that we encounter in the Gospels do modern Western Christians most resemble? He answered unhesitatingly 'the Pharisees'. I was quite shocked at the time, but now when I think about it, it seems almost self-evident. Are we like John the Baptist and the Essenes?—no, we are not desert people: there is hardly a trace of asceticism among us and we are proud of it. The Zealots then? Heavens no! Revolutionary politics is the last thing that we are into. Are we the poor to whom the good news is preached? I do not think so. Poor Christians are in the Global South. Are we like the disciples? Possibly, but on the whole we are much more interested in salvation than discipleship, with some honourable exceptions such as the Mennonites and the Anabaptists.

The Professor was probably right. We are like the Pharisees—good, earnest, respectable folk, familiar with the Scriptures, elect (i.e. not like other people), concerned about all sorts of 'purity codes', particularly purity of doctrine. We could press this a little further. The Pharisees are the Evangelicals, the Sadducees are the liberals—a bit too reductionist and rationalistic for their own good—but, if truth be told, both coming from the same stable. The Scribes are the academics and clergy perhaps; always telling people what they should do, but seldom doing it themselves.

Fundamentally what Jesus had against the religious leaders of his day was not that they were religious but that they used their religion as a cloak for injustice.

> 'Woe to you Pharisees. For you tithe mint and rue and herbs of all kinds and neglect justice and the love of God.'
> (Luke 11:42)

> 'Beware of the scribes, who like to walk around in long robes, and love to be greeted with respect in the marketplaces, and to have the best seats in the synagogues and the places of honour at banquets. They devour widows' houses and for the sake of appearance say long prayers.'
> (Luke 20:46,7)

God requires justice first and religion a long way second. Religious people like the Pharisees did not like to be reminded of this and their spiritual children are no different. John Lilburne, the seventeenth century Puritan radical attacked the religious establishment of his day in these words:

> 'And if any gilded or varnished Scribe or Pharisee...find themselves aggrieved, I desire to let them know that *fiat justitia ruat coelum*

(let justice be done though the heavens fall)
is my motto, and if I perish, it shall be in the
following of justice for justice' sake.'

The Biblical idea of justice provides us with a key to effective discipleship and the church's mission. 'Justice' is the term used in the first Servant Song (in Isaiah 42) where the Servant's task is to 'bring forth justice' and Matthew applies this passage directly to Jesus (Matthew 12:18-21) with particular reference to his ministry in Galilee.

We sometimes fail to recognise the importance of the idea because the key words in the Biblical languages have a wider meaning than our English word 'justice'. The force of the concept in both OT and NT is that justice is always *interventionary*. It is not an abstract concept, and a judge is not only someone who offers an impartial verdict having heard the evidence, but one who intervenes on behalf of the oppressed, those who are already being unfairly treated, or who are helpless in the face of powers that are too strong for them. Yahweh is the judge *for* the oppressed Israelites as well as *of* the Egyptian oppressors at the Exodus (Exodus 6:6). He is not one who waits for the outcome in order, as I say, to give an impartial verdict. He comes down and gets involved 'rolls up his sleeves and gets his hands dirty'.

The judges in the book of Judges are called 'judges' precisely because Yahweh appoints them to rescue Israel from their oppressors. In Isaiah God puts His Spirit upon his Servant so that he may bring justice to the nations. In a universal extension this means salvation for the nations and mercy to the oppressed.

God himself sends forth his justice as a light for the peoples (51:4) that will mean deliverance and salvation for them (51:5). Jesus' role is to minister to 'the bruised reed' and 'the smouldering wick' and, in restoring them, 'lead justice to victory' (Matthew 12:20). In the humiliation of the cross Jesus' justice is taken away so that he might restore it to those who did not have it (Acts 8:33 quoting Isaiah 53:8). Seen in this way justice is 'the good news to the poor' (Luke 4:18); it is God's deliverance. Not in any abstract sense, but because Jesus is proclaiming Jubilee Year, 'the year of the Lord's acceptance'.

> 'The Lord has made himself known, He has executed justice... for the needy shall not always be forgotten' (Psalm 9:16,18).

Understanding the character of God as deliverer of the oppressed is to know who God really is. We really get to know God, not so much in the place of quiet and retreat but when we participate with him in the work of deliverance in 'bringing forth justice'. There is an instructive oracle that Jeremiah delivers to King Jehoiakim. The King had been building a palace for himself by forced labour and Jeremiah scathingly contrasts his behaviour with that of his father 'good king Josiah'. We read about this in Jeremiah 22:13-16. Notice the punch line.

> Woe to him who builds his house by unrighteousness and his upper rooms by injustice; who makes his neighbours work for nothing and does not give them wages, who says 'I will build myself a spacious

> house with large upper rooms', and who cuts
> out windows for it, panelling it with cedar,
> and painting it with vermillion. Are you a
> king because you compete in cedar? Did not
> your father eat and drink and do justice and
> righteousness? Then it was well with him.
> He judged the cause of the poor and needy;
> then it was well. Is not this to know me?
> says the Lord.

I remember going to a conference on 'knowing God'. One talk was on 'knowing God in Scripture', another on 'knowing God in the quiet place'. Somebody, a missionary from India, told us a story about being in Delhi bus station. There was a woman in obvious physical distress, her sari covering her face, writhing and groaning, in the grip of some fearsome, perhaps contagious, illness, and on the whole people were avoiding her—too embarrassed or fearful, or perhaps just not wanting to be involved. We might say that helping that woman, giving her a drink, getting her to a safe place, finding some medical care, was what the Bible calls 'bringing forth justice'. But for our missionary friend it was, she recalled, supremely a time for 'knowing God'. God was there in a way that she had never experienced before.

On the basis of this we can make a number of assertions. The 'justice site', the place where we are found 'doing justice', is where we meet God. Speaking out about injustice, standing up for the poor, taking a stand on justice issues are, taken together, a description of the Christian mission. It is our mission because it is Jesus' mission, which is God's mission, *missio dei*.

What we also have to say is that God's mission seen from our perspective is context specific. It is time bound, part of history, part of *our* history. We 'know God' by discovering what is our part in the divine drama, and playing it. Jesus blamed the Jewish leaders in his day for not 'interpreting the present time'. (See Luke 12:54-6, also Matthew 16:1-4 and Luke 19:41-4.) They did not perceive that the nation was heading for disaster and it was their responsibility to steer it away from it. Their lack of perception was spiritual blindness, hypocrisy, and hardness of heart and Jesus wept about this situation (Luke19:41). This was not a matter ultimately of discernment. They knew what to do but did not want to obey; because it might mean a loss of privilege and power.

But that was *their* context and *their* task. Others have to serve their generation, to be weather fore-casters of the storm that is blowing in on them.

- For Abraham it was leaving Ur and the adventure of faith

- For the prophets it was the issue of religion and righteousness

- For Haggai and Zechariah it was the rebuilding of the temple

- For Paul it was the mission to the Gentiles

- For Luther it was preaching justification by faith

- For Carey it was 'attempting great things for God' in India

- For Christians in Nazi Europe it was the question of their Jewish neighbour

- For white South African Christians it was apartheid

- For Christians today it may be ...

Each day, as we have seen, has its issue. Not yesterday's issues or my neighbour's task. It is no use going to Israel or Palestine today and not talking politics, or to South America and not being concerned about poverty. For each one of us this is *the eye of the needle, the narrow road.* To turn aside from this task is the double-mindedness of which James speaks, it is the lame excuse of the man who hid his talent, it is the worship of the beast.

I have been reading and thinking recently about the history of the Jewish tragedy in Nazi Europe—books about the fate of the Jews in Vienna after the *Anschluss*; (Singer 2003) about Louis Darquier who was responsible for the internment and transportation of Jews from France to the concentration camps (Callil 2007); about the Italian Primo Levi who survived Auschwitz (Levi 1987), and so on. Here in Europe our response to Fascism (at least up to 1945) was 'the eye of the needle'. It pointed up, in a dramatic way, that there were choices to be made to do with fundamental justice issues.

But perhaps we can stay at that particular moment in history too long. We Brits, at least, feel rather pleased with ourselves about the Nazi episode and the second world war. After all, we like to think we were partners in a great coalition that overthrew tyranny and delivered freedom. But what about the Atlantic slave trade, or the near extermination of the indigenous population of Australia, or the exploitation of India, or the concentration camps in Kenya during the Mau Mau episode? More important even than re-imagining our own history is to ask what is the big justice issue of today?

I have struggled to find a single word to sum up today's situation. In the end I settled for 'economic imperialism'. We think the age of imperialism is over, but that is only because we come from nations that benefited from imperialism and now want to forget the fact. It would be better to ask the world's poor whether they think the age of imperialism is over. The point about imperialism is that it creates an ideology of centre and periphery that very much shapes our world today.

Let me illustrate. I used to be on the advisory board for a mission outfit called 'Servants to Asia's Urban Poor'. What a great name! Except that we might substitute 'the World' for 'Asia', it seems to me just about right. Jesus said that he was 'among us as one who serves'(Luke 22:27). It is Jesus the Servant who 'brings forth justice'. Servants are the exact opposite of imperialists. They are not at all the ones with the wealth, power and influence. 'Urban' is good because it is our actual context. Most of us live and work in cities. And then it is the poor to whom the good news is preached. What better place to start?

Let us look at urban mission. It is not, of course, that the countryside is all right. In fact one of the reasons why people are flocking into cities is to escape the crisis of the countryside. But I do believe that just at the moment cities deserve our special attention. They are, sociologically speaking, today's 'perfect storm'.

> 'One billion people—or one in three urban residents—now live in an urban slum, the vast majority of them in developing nations',

writes Mark Kramer, in his book simply called *Dispossessed, Life in our World's Urban Slums* (Kramer 2006). He adds,

> 'At current rates, within a decade of this writing we'll have more than twenty cities in the world with more than ten million inhabitants, most of them in poor nations. By the 2030s, the number of people living in informal settlements could double to about two billion, and we've yet to find some programmatic panacea for urban blight.'

Mike Davis, in his even more depressing book, *Planet of Slums* (Davis 2006) reckons that by 2015 there will be at least 550 cities with a population of more than a million. City population will be something like 10 billion by 2050. Most of these people will be living in slums and most of them will be in developing countries. The uncomfortable truth is that the modern megacity (and there are more and more of them, as we have seen) is what it is because it is a space created by economic imperialism in nearly every aspect of its relationships.

Historically, of course, many of the world's great cities such as Kolkata and Mumbai in India or Shanghai and Hong Kong in China, or Nairobi in Kenya, were the direct product of colonialism. But it is more serious than that. Any Empire essentially operates as a metropolitan centre with a subservient, contributing periphery. So does the megacity. It has a metropolitan centre where power and wealth reside and a 'colonial' periphery which can be either the rural vicinity or its own slums or both. Actually, it has a third 'periphery', a pool of immigrant labour, people who come to work in the city on 'neo-colonial' terms and who have been 'produced' by economic imperialism and its unfair economic and trading arrangements.

Here is another way of looking at it. In Matthew 11, Jesus has something to say about violence. He remarks, rather enigmatically, that 'from the days of John the Baptist until now the kingdom of heaven has suffered violence, and the violent take it by force' (v. 12). This statement comes straight after John's question about whether Jesus really is the Messiah and perhaps Jesus is saying that John never understood the principle of non-violence. Jesus' method, the way by which he is establishing his rule, is the way of healing and good news to the poor (4,5), and John may have thought that this was an inadequate response to the crisis of the day (v.6). So Jesus goes on to describe his ministry as hidden from 'the wise and the intelligent' (v.25). The kingdom has indeed come: he claims, in verse 27, that 'all things have been handed over to me by my Father', but this is *because* he has accepted the non-violent way of bringing in the kingdom. The Messianic secret is precisely this. The kingdom does not come through violence but through service. He finishes the discourse by inviting people to come to him on this basis: serving him is 'easy' and 'light' because he is 'gentle' and 'humble' (vs. 29,30).

The juxtaposition of Jesus and John the Baptist draws us back to chapter 3 and the Servant King. Jesus at his baptism is 'anointed' with texts from Psalm 2 and Isaiah 42—the kingly Psalm and the Servant Song. Psalm 2 speaks about the coronation of the king by Yahweh.

> I will tell the decree of the Lord: He said to me, 'You are my son; today (i.e. on coronation day) I have begotten you. Ask of me, and I will make the nations your inheritance.'
> (Psalm 2:7,8)

There is a secret here that will 'win the nations'. Notice however, that in Matthew chapter 4 someone else is promising the same 'inheritance'. 'All of these [the kingdoms of the world] I will give you, if you will fall down and worship me' says Satan (v.8). So what was the difference? Satan's method was power through miracle and magic. Jesus would be seen as the new Moses giving manna in the wilderness, as the Messiah who 'suddenly comes to his temple' as in Malachi (3:1). It was a sort of prosperity Gospel and mass rally miracle combined into one. And we see plenty of people today trying to 'bring in the kingdom' by these dubious methods. Perhaps we have used them ourselves. But Jesus had already been told what sort of kingdom it was, and what sort of king it was, about whom God could say 'I am well pleased'.

As we have already noted, in Matthew chapter 12 we get another specific reference to Isaiah 42 (12:18-21), to the Servant who proclaims and establishes justice, specifically justice for the 'bruised reed' and the 'smouldering wick'. It is in that sort of king that 'the nations will put their hope', again a universal and missiological reference. The quotation implies, among other things, that justice is the key to the process of establishing the kingdom.

The first part of chapter 12 is about justice for those who were oppressed by the purity and debt system, something which the Pharisees thought worth maintaining by violence. (Verse 14 says that it was at this point that they planned to destroy Jesus.) Verse 8 indicates that the issue has to do with the authority of the new king ('the Son of Man is lord of the Sabbath') who desires 'mercy and not sacrifice' (vs. 7,8). The issue of authority and power is very much to the fore here (v.24). Perhaps the comment of the Pharisees was not as cynical or dismissive as we think. It may be that they really thought that Jesus had tapped into a system of power they needed to exploit. But Jesus was operating under a completely different regime.

We, like the scribes and Pharisees, sometimes think that the only way we can defeat the opposition is by displaying greater power, by dipping into the same sources of power that the System employs, only doing it better. So if the Enemy builds a big building, we will build a bigger church. If the opposition floods the locality with their holy book, we will multiply the availability of Bibles. If they are zealous we will be more zealous. An apt commentary on all this would be Zechariah's word to Zerubbabel 'not by might, nor by power, but by my spirit, says the Lord' (Zechariah 4:6).

Jesus' inauguration of the kingdom was 'by the Spirit' (v.28) and we know that the Spirit anoints Jesus not for a power contest but for justice and mercy (vs. 18-20). We should notice that Jesus is very concerned about the *source* of ministry in this chapter (vs. 33-35). The key issue is to do with *attitudes* rather than end product. Seeking a sign (v.38) is once again coming from the wrong angle. There is a sign, but it is the sign of apparent failure, of seclusion and death (v.40). Further the wrong use of power, even when initially successful, leads to greater corruption (vs. 43-5), and this is a corporate rather than individual reference.

It is not of course that nothing is happening. The Kingdom is not simply the negation of Empire. Jesus is at pains to teach that something new and 'great' is being revealed: greater than the Temple (v.6), greater than Jonah (v.41), greater than Solomon (v.42): a new priest, prophet and king has arrived. But the newness is a matter of obedient relationship in a new community (vs. 49,50). The confrontation also links with Matthew chapter 23 where the scribes and the Pharisees are accused of injustice because of the way that they use the System (as above) (vs. 4, 23 etc.) and once again violence is very much part of the picture (vs. 34-6). The immediate contrast is Jesus' ministry— a hen gathering her chicks (v.37).

Economic imperialism and its offspring neo-colonialism are essentially violent. If we were to discern its interiority (as Jesus did when he healed the Gadarene demoniac—a story which is about colonial occupation and is full of violence) then we would encounter a violent spirit. Not just the violence of military hardware and economic injustice (a mobile phone works because it has crucial metallurgic components over the mining of which there have been extensive wars in Africa), but also the violence of cultural and linguistic imperialism and 'superior' knowledge.

Often we need to begin with the violence in our own hearts and the imperialistic attitudes we find there. We are, it may be, too clever to hear what is being revealed to babies, too impatient to accept Jesus' gentle yoke, too ready to 'break the bruised reed' and 'quench the smouldering wick', too enamoured of miracle and magic (today it would be the technological fix) to enter into the true inheritance that belongs to the Messiah and his people: in a word too violent.

Of course, it is dangerously easy at his stage to be disempowered by our guilt. Jesus renounced the violence of Empire, but he was not passive or resigned. In a practical and even hard-headed way we need to access anti-imperial ways of thinking and then adopt anti-imperial behaviour. Too much of our mission is still wedded to the Enlightenment Project expressed as imperialism; it is this imperial 'violence' which we must renounce. I grew up with the relentless myth of Progress, which seemed more and more as time passed to be simply untrue. I floundered about for a long time but I never really felt at ease with my own world view until I encountered the Critical Theorists and, in particular, Walter Benjamin. What they enabled me to do was to become a civilisational pessimist while remaining an existential optimist, to believe that God is still in control and that 'all will be well', but also to be allowed to abandon any idea that we are aiming at progress or success.

In fact the Gospel takes a consistent stand against what might be called the violence of progress, that is the use of power and the offer of success to build an empire. It is the opposite of empires, hierarchy, establishment, orthodoxy, fixed arrangements, essentialism, authoritarianism, prescription, triumphalism etc. It is on the side of freedom, hybridity, suspicion, description, performance, interpretation, narrative, subaltern memory, flexibility, imagination, radicality etc. Furthermore it collapses the whole binary system altogether—no more 'us' and 'them', male and female, slave or free, Jew and Gentile—i.e. patriarchy, class superiority, race superiority: gender, social class and ethnicity used as a power mechanism in a divided world.

How then should we live? What does justice demand? In all these matters we must not be prepared to wait. There is urgency! We must *leave*. (Remember Lot's wife!) The challenge to God's people is always to leave Empire to go out to where God is, whether the Empire is Egypt, Babylon, Rome or today's global empire. Leaving, in this sense, is *integral* to mission.

Then there is the challenge to *belong*, to begin to build a new community. There is no doubt that Jesus offered the people of his day 'the alternative community', (a *just* community; see Matthew 6:33). A community of people under the Lordship of Christ is still how the Kingdom of God is best demonstrated today: it is 'the sign of the Kingdom'. Community building is the ultimate task in the fight against injustice, as long, that is, that we are speaking of God's community, not ours. The New Jerusalem comes down (present continuous tense) out of heaven *from God* (Rev. 21:2). It is God's invention, the masterpiece of *missio dei*.

Oddly enough, this should make us pause in our programmes of evangelism and church planting and the like. Why? Because God is already at work building his Kingdom, in every context, even before the Church comes along. The Church makes the Kingdom visible, and introduces the King. This makes me suspicious of anything we do in the name of the Gospel which destroys community.

The purpose of the New Jerusalem is that there should be 'a dwelling of God among people' and we read that the nations bring their riches into the city and that 'the leaves of the tree—i.e. the tree of life in Main Street, New Jerusalem—are for the healing of the nations.' We have some powerful biblical images here. We have already mentioned the city but there is also a garden. A garden is a garden because it is neither a jungle on one hand nor a concrete space on the other; it is neither wholly natural nor is it entirely artificial. Justice is best served when we are aiming, may I suggest, at horticulture or gardening ('my Father is the gardener'). In a garden there is life: it may need directing, but it is not a question of destruction. Perhaps too often our mission methods have been accompanied by a trampling disregard for the forms of life already existing.

Also, we must beware that we do not turn gardening or agriculture into agribusiness. In our world today this is usually done in the name of *production*. But though God is interested in fruitfulness (Colossians 1:6) he is not really that interested in numbers. Jesus turned away from the crowds and kept on 'cultivating' his close disciples. In the name of productivity we humans have all too often turned a fruitful field into a barren wilderness. Just look around.

How do we destroy a community? Well, as Simone Weil has said, money will do it soon enough (Weil 2002,44). But there are certainly other enemies: the love of power for one, as we have seen. Power games go deep into our psyche. (This is often, but not always, linked with money.) Many of our Christian leadership courses go wrong at precisely this point. We teach leadership in such a way that it is intended to enhance our ability to exercise power, to enhance our control. But, is that the right approach? 'I am among you as one who serves' said Jesus. In the end we have come full circle. Violence, power hunger, imperialism are as natural to us as the air we breathe. In the Kingdom, however, the power belongs to God not to us. 'Your kingdom come. Yours is the power and the glory.'

If you take the two principles that we have been working with—firstly that justice means intervention on behalf of the 'losers', and secondly that the critical determinant of specific action is the context—then you have a working model for mission. I would only add that we need to look at this on a variety of scales. Justice in the story of the Good Samaritan was precisely to do with responding to the need of the man lying by the roadside. He required 'intervention' and the Jericho Road was the context—it 'set the agenda' as they say. A modern example would be my missionary in the Delhi bus station. But at another level structural injustice requires structural intervention. There are 'yokes of bondage' which need smashing. It could be King Jehoiakim using forced labour as in Jeremiah 22, or it could be the generals in Myanmar who are currently using similar methods to build their country villas and golf courses. At a mega scale, Jesus attacked the purity code and the debt system of the Jewish Temple state which kept the rich rich and the poor poor; today it might be the unfair trading system which currently operates between the West and the Global South and which has the same effect. Or, to put it slightly differently, one issue—street children for example—may have a number of levels. The child on the street whom I encounter every day on my way to work is one challenge. The police action against street children which may go so far as a 'shoot on sight' policy, would demand urgent action of another sort. An investigation as to why there are so many children on the streets would be a further, wider issue. All of these are *justice* issues in the Biblical sense. My own particular circumstances, my context, would determine which issue or issues I addressed.

It might be good, in the light of this, if, we were to respond to this demand for context by drawing up a map of 'injustice sites' for our generation. I do this in an attempt to be rooted and practical and not because I think the list is definitive or because I think I can find other disciples' guidance for them! Rather the examples below are paradigmatic and personal. Here is a first attempt.

- Prisons

- Work places for the economically vulnerable

- Areas of ethnic or racial tension

- War zones

- Families, especially those under patriarchal arrangements.

I suspect that in most (perhaps all) prisons there are people who should not be there at all or are there for an unreasonable amount of time; they have not had a fair trial, or the law has been too harsh. Some have been justly sentenced but are being unjustly treated by the prison authorities or the other inmates. Then there are those who are there as the victims of political repression, or religious persecution, or social prejudice. Some have landed up in prison and then have simply been forgotten. Within prison gates, people are treated as less than human (the widespread use of solitary confinement comes to mind) or there is inadequate control, with the weaker members being subject to violence they cannot avoid.

The economically vulnerable (aka 'the poor') are always in danger of being unjustly treated by the rich and powerful—their property may be unfairly seized, their land occupied, their rights disregarded in the courts, and so on. The workplace, however, provides us with many of the best (or worst) examples of injustice. In general farm labourers (as distinct from landowners) have often been paid very little for their work, and that is still true today in many countries. Similarly the whole history of the industrial revolution is littered with stories of low wages, long working hours, and poor conditions. The factories and mines of the nineteenth century are legendary in this respect. Today's equivalents are the sweatshops of the new expanding economies of the Global South, producing goods at 'competitive' prices to be sold to the already relatively well-off middle classes of their own and other nations. Nor is this the only example. Immigrant labour is exploited in wealthy Western countries. Sex workers are exploited everywhere. Many countries are unable or unwilling to prevent exploitive child labour. Factors of class and caste and race still make it difficult for people to earn a decent living. Even in wealthy countries, the minimum wage is pitifully low.

We like to think of our world as increasingly tolerant of 'difference', more willing to affirm 'the other', more willing to be multi-cultural, in a word less prejudiced. It may be so, though taking all things into consideration, the twentieth century did not have a very good record. The twenty-first century has yet to reveal its real colours. Be that as it may, there are plenty of places where to be the wrong colour, race, religion or language group is to face daily injustice and frequent danger. Once these dangers break out into the open, with riots, looting, destruction of property and even massacres, then justice is largely forgotten. People side with their own kin whatever the rights and wrongs of the situation and the authorities do the same. When matters are reduced in this way to the law of the jungle then it is very hard to prevent the growth of multiple sites of injustice. Where people once lived happily and peacefully together there is now division, with the 'minorities' typically the losers.

Little needs to be said about the injustices that war brings because it is all too painfully obvious. War is a great evil. Quite apart from huge resources being invested in death and destruction; quite apart from the way the participants are brutalised and traumatised; quite apart from its inevitable legacy of hatred and revenge, a war zone is a place where all the rules of civilised behaviour, including rules of fairness and reciprocity, are set aside. As a result everybody suffers. Even good people are corrupted by war, as we saw when quite ordinary men and women did abominable things at Abu Ghraib. Even innocent people, perhaps especially innocent people, suffer alongside the warmongers. Justice never gets a look in.

In some ways injustice within families is the saddest example of them all. Whatever we think about family life it is certainly intended to provide mutual support for parents and a safe place for children to grow up in. Yet, because of the intimacy that is a necessary characteristic of being a family, it is also a place wide open to abuse of power and a great variety of injustices. Husbands knock their wives about (and occasionally vice versa) with impunity. Children are physically ill-treated and psychologically damaged. Cruelties abound. The situation is made worse by patriarchal attitudes in society at large, so that in many cultures the husband and father's bad behaviour is sanctioned by custom and the law.

These sites of injustice should be of special concern to Christians, simply because of the character of the God we serve. It should make us passionately angry that there are so many injustices associated with our prisons, our workplaces, our 'mixed' communities, our armies and even our families. But anger should lead to action. What can we do about it?

First of all we must be sure that we are not directly involved in injustice ourselves. We may be paying unnecessarily meagre wages, working for the military establishment, or dominating our families in an oppressive way. Much more likely is that we are benefiting from injustices carried out by others, but, so to speak, on our behalf. What about buying cheap goods which can only be cheap because they are produced by poorly paid workers? Then there are those who support others who are clearly discriminating against immigrants for fear that they might come and live on our streets or take our jobs. Again, we give our taxes for the purchase of weapons that we know are going to harm innocent civilians, because we put our security above their welfare. All of these stand on the negative side. But is there also an active response?

Prisons

None of us live far away from a prison. I wonder whether we know what is going on 'behind bars' in our own town? Are there any children there, for example? Children can be tried and imprisoned in the UK at the age of ten (four years younger than China and six years younger than in Texas). We have more child prisoners than any other country in Europe[28]. Again, are conditions in prison such that people learn how to be criminals in prison? Certainly our recidivism rates (95% for young adult males) suggest that there is not much emphasis on reform as against punishment[29]. In the past prison reform was largely the

28 See the article by George Monbiot in *Guardian 29/06/2010.*
29 ibid

work of Christian pressure groups. Is that something that might happen again?

Of course, there is more to it than what is happening in our prisons. We need just laws. We need a good police force and conscientious lawyers and judges. In general imprisonment rates are not determined by crime rates so much as by differences in official attitudes which favour punishment as against rehabilitation and reform. In the UK we imprison 124 people per 100,000 as against 40 per 100,000 in Japan, and in recent years our prison population has been rising rapidly (1990: 46,000, 2007: 80,000) [30]. Both of these figures largely reflect the demand of the public for more punishment rather than the outcome of a rising number of offences. So what about us, I mean us Christians, as members of the public? What are we demanding? Even more generally, we need to ask the bigger social questions: why do people get into trouble with the law in the first place, and who looks after them when they get out of prison.

The Workplace

The workplace scene is rather different depending on whether we are employers or employed. We have already mentioned the need to pay good wages as an employer and 'good' wages probably means more than the minimum wage! Obviously we also have to strive to be fair in terms of assigning work hours and duties, not to mention promotions and the

30 These statistics and a wealth of other useful information about imprisonment and punishment can be found in Wilkinson and Pickett 2010.

like. It is depressing that so many people hate their work and would get out if they could afford to do so, while there are many who would be happy to do any sort of work—if they could get it. Similarly, many are depressed and anxious because they cannot find employment, while an equal number are stressed by being asked to work at a rate they cannot sustain. Employers are not necessarily directly responsible for this state of affairs, but they may be able to help. A good employer can insist that his or her employees do not work too hard, can take on extra help for over pressed staff (even if this adds to the wage packet) and can treat staff equally whatever their roles in the organisation. Christians who are running their own businesses can think about moving towards co-operative arrangements by which all have a stake in the enterprise. This tends to flatten out wage differentials, mitigates the feeling that employees often have that they do all the work and the boss gets all the profits, and increases people's work satisfaction as they feel a growing sense of ownership. Employees, especially in big firms, should join their Union and if necessary play an active part in it.

It is not generally recognised how much the Trade Union movement has done, in Britain for example, to promote justice in the workplace, and how much we still need the sort of protection the Unions offer. We heard a great deal, particularly in the Thatcher era, about the way the Unions were abusing their power, but we do not have to go back very far into the history of industrial relations to realise how much injustice there was when employers had things all their own way. Even the period of supposed Union dominance—

after post-war austerity and before the Miners' Strike—was a time, now sadly gone, when the gap between the rich and the poor was steadily diminishing: a sure sign that, perhaps the only sign, that, in terms of industrial relations, the country was becoming a fairer place. It is extraordinary how Christian people can fail to see how this matters.

Being active in Trade Union affairs is not the only possibility of promoting fairness as an employee. We can stand up for people who are being bullied, protest against discrimination, point out to the authorities where people are being exploited, set an example by not trying to curry favour with the boss, insist on democratic procedures, be prepared to accept lower wages as an alternative to (someone else's) redundancy—there are many opportunities. Injustice is usually at its worst when a firm or organisation is in survival mode. 'Powers' (any corporate enterprise) are intended by God to serve people, but the minute their ultimate goal is survival then they start exploiting people. The Christian testimony is—even if that Christian is only a humble employee—that justice comes first, even before survival. So my company is never god. Its survival is never the most important consideration, and that includes times when my own job is at stake. As a Christian I am not permitted to neglect my family, ruin my health, distance myself from other legitimate commitments for the sake of my job. That is one of the meanings of not attending to the Sabbath rest, but more straightforwardly simply a case of serving mammon rather than God.

One of my favourite stories in this respect is of a young law graduate who was beginning his first job at a prestigious law firm. On his first day at work he mentioned to his new boss that he had just got married. Indeed it was his new job that had made him feel sufficiently financially secure to do this. 'Oh', said the boss, 'if you intended to get married you should have told us. It's the sort of thing we expect to know.' And then he added: 'and don't even think of having any children. You certainly won't have time for that.' It is easy to see how wrong this is, how the company is already beginning to assume that in return for a no doubt decent salary, it has 'bought' its new employee body and soul. But my main point here is that it is the newly employed young man who needs to stand up for justice in this situation. His big temptation will be to go along with things: 'I can't kick up a fuss on my very first day at work,' he will be saying to himself. But the danger is that before very long he will have slipped into the corporate ethos himself. Christians need to protest against this sort of wickedness, whenever and wherever it occurs, if they are to retain a good conscience. Nor are they just standing up for their own rights; rather they are challenging the whole ethos of the group under which many others may well be suffering.

Racial and Ethnic Tension

What can we do as Christians when we are aware that in our own neighbourhood there are evident cases of discrimination against ethnic and religious groups? At one simple level it would be a good start to have a number of friends and acquaintances from among them. This in itself raises the issue of language: learning a little Bengali or Polish, or helping my new friends to improve their English. Reading up about the appropriate cultures might similarly help. This could be more than simply trying to avoid cultural blunders. Whoever my friends are, they feel supported by others who take a genuine interest in them, and who listen to their stories with a measure of understanding and enthusiasm. I worked for many years in India and have an interest in keeping up with Indian affairs. When I meet Indians working in this country they sometimes comment on how little there is in the British press about India. They also seem pleased and surprised when they find that I know the name of India's Prime Minister, that I know who the Naxalites are and that I have read *The White Tiger* (Adiga 2008). For them it is a form of injustice that the greater part of their life's experience does not seem to have any meaning for the people among whom they have come to live. We can try to change this.

Here in Britain many of the injustices suffered by our ethnic minorities have to do with their status as immigrants. They are subject to another sort of 'power', the power of discriminatory thought, a way of thinking that is essentially unjust and which is often fostered by the media. It is also largely irrational but not less pernicious because of that. It is the task of Christians to undo this sort of thinking by every means possible. We can begin by combating the idea that there is something wrong with being a migrant. (Certainly the term 'economic migrant' has such connotations.) It is gross hypocrisy on the part of the British, for example, to accuse people of the 'crime' of wanting to move to another country in order to better their standard of living. People have always done this since human history began, but in our case for a number of centuries we British emigrated to all parts of the world—notably North America, Australasia and parts of Africa, and usually for economic reasons. Even in recent years there has been a considerable outflow of British people to the European Continent, especially Spain. In a sense, everybody who has moved, even from Leeds to London, to get a better job, is an economic migrant.

The last time I mentioned the inconvenient fact of nineteenth century European (especially British) emigration to somebody who was taking a prejudicial attitude to migrants in Britain, they suggested that there was a significant difference: that in the nineteenth century the countries they migrated to were empty. Well, no, actually. There were people there, but the usual idea was to exterminate them, of if that were not entirely possible, to subjugate them. This does raise a point, however. Migrants coming to this country today are always in a minority in terms of ethnicity, religion and culture (and that includes language). Now God likes minorities, because he likes diversity (see Revelation 7: 9) and where there is diversity there will be minorities. Minorities are almost always in a weak position in a given community, and that is another reason why God is on their side, and why we Christians should be also. Indeed, I would say that we Christians have no choice.

There are two ways that we can respond to these minorities. One is to help them to integrate and the other is to affirm their difference. It is unjust to demand that everybody should be like us. But equally many of the injustices that they will experience are because their religion, culture and language place them at a disadvantage when dealing with the majority culture. Narrowing the cultural gap in practical ways is 'justice work'. I have already mentioned the language gap, but there are other ways, such as explaining our bureaucracy, that can be part of this process.

Asylum seekers are often numbered with the immigrants. They are often simply thought of as people from abroad who want to stay, without any consideration of the dangers from which they have escaped and to which they might return if repatriated. Here we might want to be sure that the laws are being applied fairly, providing, that is, that we think that we have just asylum laws and procedures in the first place, something else we should be looking into. Perhaps it is difficult for ordinary citizens, which is what most Christians are, to be too certain about such matters, but we can at least be especially willing to befriend any asylum seekers that God sends to us. In my own, admittedly rather limited, experience, the asylum seekers I have encountered have all been people who, to put it rather simplistically, deserved to *stay*. However, no doubt each case needs to be judged on its own merits. The unjust situation would be if there were a presupposition that most asylum seekers were not what they claimed to be and deserved to go, to be repatriated.

If this is in fact the climate of opinion, then we must try to change it. The proprietors and journalists attached to certain well known newspapers have much to answer for in creating just such wrong attitudes, and Christians should be buying and reading something else.

War

I do not believe that there is such a thing as a just war either in theory or practice, though there may be a war which is the lesser of two evils. I am not even sure about that. I certainly think that every possible non-violent approach must be investigated by Christians before they join the warriors. I also think that going to war against another nation is only ever justified if it is conducted under the aegis of some other supervising body that has no direct gain from the outcome. (I have written about this elsewhere and will pursue it no further here.)

As we have said, justice is an early casualty in a war zone. Perhaps the best we can do as Christians is to persistently undercut the way that war is marketed and glamorised. If war is at best a necessary evil it should be treated as such with the emphasis on *evil*. Military action should be seen as on a par with jobs that need to be done because things have gone wrong, but also seen as something which nobody in their right mind would do under normal everyday circumstances. Also, we must resist the way that our society is constantly increasing the number of war zones. 'The war on drugs' and 'the war on terror' are two obvious examples. What this sort of thinking enables people to do is to tear up the normal rules and to act unjustly with impunity. Think of the use of torture, the targeting of suspects (they cannot be anything more) with death-dealing drones, the use of indefinite imprisonment without trial, the wholesale invasions of privacy, and all in the name of a war which is no such thing. We know that people do wicked things (9/11!) and they must be prevented from doing so if possible and certainly brought to justice when they have done so. We appoint police and judges to do this on our behalf. We have appointed them to *uphold* the rule of law, because there are elements in our society who are determined not to keep the law.

If, however, we dispense with our own laws, then we have made a naked appeal to power—which is when justice disappears. We know that this is a disaster because even in war we try to impose rules—the treatment of prisoners of war, for example, is the subject of an international agreement. Two things might be said about this, however. Most accounts of actual warfare give me the impression that the rules of war are widely disregarded when it comes to the battlefield. Secondly, the so-called 'war on terror' seems to have dispensed with these rules. The inmates of Guantanamo Bay have been denied even prisoner of war status.

So we Christians need to minimise the incidence of war in whatever way we can. We should refuse to fight in the case of an 'unjust war' and protest against the government if it is waging it in our name. We should not usually be involved in the manufacture and distribution of weapons of war. If we work for the intelligence services we should insist that they too keep the laws. We should stop behaving as if war was something glamorous. (This has wide implications for the way history is taught in our schools, the content of the media, the toys or clothes we buy our children, and so on.) We should object every time the phrase 'the war on terror' is used, demanding that we go back to a time when we relied on our police and intelligence services to protect us, in the understanding that they were our servants, as much subject to the law of the land as the rest of us.

Families

We all know that there are injustices just below the surface in many families and this applies to Christian families too. These injustices can take many forms: unequal relationships between partners, unfair demands on children, neglect of parents, favouritism, lack of appreciation, exploitation, even cruelty and abuse in the face of vulnerability. It is particularly sad when these practices are given divine sanction: patriarchal attitudes are justified by reference to the Bible, children are beaten with the same excuse, others are cowed by religious threats and so on. It is bad enough that people are made to suffer injustice. It is even worse when they are told that the injustice is God's will.

'Bringing forth justice' presents so many challenges that sometimes it all seems impossibly daunting. When we look at the example of Jesus and our key text in Matthew chapter 12, it is notable that one of the reasons why Matthew chose the description from Isaiah 42 was because it did not portray Jesus' ministry in terms of the big event, the dramatic entry, widespread publicity or powerful 'evangelism'. Indeed success did not really seem to come into it. Quite the reverse. The clear understanding was that justice came in a different way. It came through faith-fulness and perseverance, through small incremental gains, through concern for needy and broken people, through a voice that was clear and firm but was never raised to a shout.

CONCLUSIONS: THE END OF ALL THINGS IS NEAR

I suppose we have all wondered from time to time whether, without knowing it, we are in the sort of world crisis that will end in disaster. Will the terrorists produce some particularly nasty surprise? Will global warming mean that changes in the climate are about to signal vast and irreversible catastrophes? Is a nuclear war still possible, and will it pollute the world's atmosphere in such a way that we are all living next to Chernobyl, so to speak? Is AIDS just the forerunner of a whole series of mass epidemics? Will the poor of the earth rise up and overturn the world order, refusing at the last to accept the huge gulf that has grown up between them and the rich, exchanging violence for impotence?

There is no doubt that we live in the context of crisis, even if usually we are insufficiently aware of it. Since the economic crash of 2008 we seem to be doing a little better (the patient has recovered somewhat, even if we do not like the medicine very much) but we are quite accepting of the fact that the next economic crisis may be just around the corner. We have become fairly adept at ignoring the environmental crisis (despite the warnings of the people, like climate scientists, who actually know what is going on) but again, few of us really believe that we can go on as we have before, borrowing and consuming the earth's resources without any thought of repayment. I have written recently about how I think we should respond to this situation[31] and I do not want to repeat myself, but I thought it worthwhile to end on a note of warning, given that this book is about context and another word for 'context' is 'environment'.

Everything that has been written here about contemporary culture, history and tradition, Christian ministry and even personal growth would sound very different if civilisation itself and we ourselves with it were suddenly thrown into a series of unprecedented disasters which threatened our very existence. We may think this alarmist, darkly apocalyptic, the stuff of nightmares rather than sober reality. After all there have always been doomsayers who have predicted the end of the world. Yes, but Magnason (see the title page) speaks about alienation as a condition in which 'people have no overview over the context in which they live their lives'[32]. Our context is not only the here-and-now, but also the way our past has formed us and *how we understand the future*.

Let me suggest a number of ways we can make this work for us.

By taking the warnings seriously. Our end of the age is perhaps similar to the one described by C.S. Lewis in *The Magician's Nephew* where Digory and Polly encounter the dying world of Charn, and are just in time to see its final destruction. The children had entered Charn by a pool in the Wood Between the Worlds, and at the end of their adventures they found themselves again in the wood.

31 See Ingleby 2010b.
32 A. S. Magnason, *Dreamland* London; Citizen Press, 2008, p. 83.

'When you were last here,' said Aslan, 'that hollow was a pool, and when you jumped into it you came to the world where a dying sun shone over the ruins of Charn. There is no pool now. That world is ended, as if it had never been. Let the race of Adam and Eve take warning.'

'Yes, Aslan,' said both the children. But Polly added, 'But we're not quite as bad as that world, are we, Aslan?'

'Not yet, Daughter of Eve,' he said. 'Not yet. But you are growing more like it. It is not certain that some wicked one of your race will not find out a secret as evil as the Deplorable Word and use it to destroy all living things. And soon, very soon, before you are an old man and an old woman, great nations in your world will be ruled by tyrants who care no more for joy and justice and mercy than Queen Jadis. Let your world beware. That is the warning.'

(Lewis 1955, 175-6)

By being more sure, as Christians of 'the hope that is within us'. What, after all, is promised to us? What is 'the hope of heaven'? What about a new heaven and earth, which is our final context?

By redoubling our efforts to live godly lives. See what the author of First Peter says *after* he has warned his readers that 'the end of all things is near':

> The end of all things is near; therefore be serious and discipline yourselves for the sake of your prayers. Above all, maintain constant love for one another, for love covers a multitude of sins. Be hospitable to one another, without complaining. Like good stewards of the manifold grace of God, serve one another with whatever gift each of you has received. Whoever speaks must do so as one speaking the very words of God, whoever serves must do so with the strength that God supplies, so that God may be glorified in all these things through Jesus Christ. To him belong the glory and the power for ever and ever. Amen.
>
> (1 Peter 4:7-11)

Much of this book is about forces and events (past and present) which bear down upon us in powerful ways whether we like it or not. Our past cannot now be changed, our context is a 'given', we certainly can do little to predict the future, let alone control it.

But this knowledge is not intended to disempower us. The better we understand these things the more we are able to shape our own lives. Alienation consists of *not* understanding them. Indeed, as we have been saying all along, 'the critical hermeneutical principle is the context'. Understanding the context gives us the key to interpreting our lives.

BIBLIOGRAPHY

Adiga 2008 Adiga, A *The White Tiger.* London: Atlantic

Allen & Thomas 1992 Allen T. and Thomas A. eds. *Poverty and Development in the 1990s* Oxford: Oxford University Press

Anderson 1998 Anderson, B. *The Spectre of Comparisons* London: Verso

Axling 1932 Axling, W. *Kagawa* London: SCM

Bartolovich 2003 Bartolovich, C. 'The Eleventh September of George Bush, Fortress US and the Global Politics of Consumption' in *Interventions* 5/2, 2003 pp. 177-99

Bauman 1993 Bauman, Z. *Postmodern Ethics* Oxford: Blackwells

Bauman 2001 Bauman, Z. *The Individualized Society* Cambridge: Polity

Bauman 2003 Bauman, Z. *Liquid Love* Cambridge: Polity

Beilharz 2000 Beilharz, P. *Zygmunt Bauman, Dialectic of Modernity*, London: Sage

Benjamin 2009 Benjamin, W. *One Way Street and Other Writings*, London: Penguin

Berry 1981   Berry, W. *Recollected Essays*, San Francisco, North Point Press*World In Context*

Berry 1993   Berry, W. *Sex, Economy, Freedom and Community* New York: Pantheon

Boyd 1969   Boyd, R. *An Introduction to Indian Christian Theology* Delhi: ISPCK

Breuggemann 1993   Breuggemann, W. *The Bible and Postmodern Imagination* London: SCM

Brook & Gwyther 2002   Brook W. & Gwyther, A. *Unveiling Empire* Maryknoll, N.J.:Orbis

Caird 1966   Caird, G.B. *The Revelation of St John the Divine*, London: A & C Black

Callil 2007   Callil, C. *Bad Faith, A Story of Faith and Fatherland* London: Vintage

Castells 1998   Castells, M. *The End of the Millennium* Oxford: Blackwell

Castells 2000   Castells, M. *The Rise of the Network Society* (Second edition), Oxford: Blackwell

Castells 2004   Castells, M. *The Power of Identity* (Second edition) Oxford: Blackwell

Cohen & Kennedy 2000 Cohen R. & Kennedy P. *Global Sociology* London: Macmillan

Curtis 2001   Curtis, M. *Trade for Life: Making Trade Work for Poor People* London; Christian Aid

Davis 2001   Davis, M. *Late Victorian Holocausts* London: Verso

Davis 2006   Davis, M. *Planet of Slums* London: Verso 288

De Zengotita 2007   De Zengotita, T. *Mediated* London: Bloomsbury

Dillard 1983   Dillard, A. *Teaching a Stone to Talk* New York: Harper and Row

Ehrenreich 2002   Ehrenreich, B. *Nickel and Dimed* London: Granta Books

Ford 1999   Ford, D. *Theology, A Very Short Introduction* Oxford: Oxford University Press

Freedman 2002   Freedman, J. 'Situating Hybridity, The Positional Logic of a Discourse' pp. 125-47 in Chew, S.C. & Knottnerus, J.D. *Structure, Culture and History, Recent Issues in Social Theory* Lanham: Rowman & Littlefield

Giddens 1999   Giddens, A. *Runaway World* London: Profile Books

Goldberg 2002   Goldberg, D. & Quayson, A. eds. *Relocating Postcolonialism*, Oxford: Blackwell

Goldsmith 2001   Goldsmith, E. & Mander, J. eds. *The Case Against the Global Economy* London: Earthscan

Gorringe 2000   Gorringe, T. 'The Shape of the Human Home: Cities, Global Capital and *Ec-clesia*' *Political Theology*, 3, Nov 2000 pp. 80-

Gray 2002   Gray, J. 'Why Terrorism is Unbeatable', *New Statesman* 25 February 2002

Gray 2010   Gray, J. *Gray's Anatomy* London: Penguin

Hardt & Negri 2000   Hardt, M. and Negri, A. *Empire*, London: Harvard University Press

Harvey 1996   Harvey, D. *Justice, Nature and the Geography of Difference* Oxford: Blackwell

Held & McGrew 1999 Held, D. & McGrew, A. et al. *Global Transformations* Cambridge: Polity

Held & McGrew 2000 Held, D. & McGrew, A. (eds.) *Global Transformations Reader*, Cambridge: Polity

Herzog 1994   Herzog II, W. *Parables as Subversive Speech* Louisville: Westminster John Knox Press

Ingleby 1997   Ingleby, J. 'Trickling Down or Shaking the Foundations: Is Contextualization Neutral?' in *Missiology* XXV, No.2 April

Ingleby 2007   Ingleby, J. 'Small Communities and the Impact of Modernity: a Meditation on Mario Vargas Llosa's *El Hablador* and its Meaning for Mission Today' in *Transformation* 24/1 January 2007

Ingleby 2010a   Ingleby, J. *Beyond Empire* Milton Keynes: Authorhouse

Ingleby 2010b   Ingleby, J. *Christians and Catastrophe* Gloucester: Wide Margin

Jameson 1992   Jameson, F. *Postmodernism, or The Cultural Logic of Late Capitalism* London: Verso

Jameson 2000　　Jameson, F. 'Globalisation and Political Strategy' in *New Left Review* 4 July/August 2000 pp. 49-68

Kellermann 1991　　Kellermann, B.W. *Seasons of Faith and Conscience*, Maryknoll: Orbis

Khor 2001　　Khor, M. *Rethinking Globalization*, London, Zed Books

Kingsnorth 2008　　Kingsnorth, P. *Real England* London: Portobello

Kovel 2002　　Kovel, J. *The Enemy of Nature* London: Zed Books

Kramer 2006　　Kramer, M. *Dispossessed, Life in our World's Urban Slums* Maryknoll: Orbis

Lechner & Boli 2000　　Lechner F. & Boli, J. *The Globalization Reader* Oxford: Blackwell

Levi 1987　　Levi, P. *If This Is A Man* London: Abacus

Lewis 1955　　Lewis, C. S. *The Magician's Nephew* London:The Bodley Head

Lundy 2002　　Lundy, J.D. *Servant Leadership* Milton Keynes: Authentic Lifestyle

Maier 2000　　Maier, K. *This House Has Fallen* London: Penguin Books

Meyer 1998　　Meyer, B. ' "Make a Complete Break with the Past": Memory and Postcolonial Modernity in Ghanaian Pentecostal Discourse'

chapter 7 in Richard Werbner, ed., *Memory and the Postcolony*, London: Zed Books

Myers 1994   Myers, C. *Who Will Roll Away the Stone?* Maryknoll: Orbis

Niebuhr 1951   Niebuhr, H. Richard *Christ and Culture* New York: Harper and Row

O'Riordan 2001   O'Riordan T. ed., *Globalism, Localism and Identity*, London: Earthscan

Pugh 1988   Pugh, M. *Lloyd George* London: Longman

Puttnam et al. 2000   Puttnam, R., Phatt S. and Dalton, R., *What is Troubling the Mature Democracies?*, Princeton: Princeton University Press

Rogers 2002   Rogers, P. *Losing Control: Global Survival in the Twenty-first Century*, Second Edition, London: Pluto Press

Rose 1996   Rose, G. *Mourning Becomes the Law, Philosophy and Representation* Cambridge: Cambridge University Press

Roy 2002   Roy, A. *The Algebra of Infinite Justice* London: Flamingo

Ruskin 1862   Ruskin J., *Sesame and Lilies* and *Unto This Last* London: Gresham, 1862

Rynne 2008   Rynne, T. *Gandhi's Jesus, The Saving Power of Nonviolence* Maryknoll: Orbis

Said 2003   Said, E. *Orientalism* (New Edition) London: Penguin

Sardar & Davies 2002 Sardar, Z. and Davies, W.M. *Why Do People Hate America?* Cambridge: Icon Books

Schaeffer 2003 Schaeffer, R. *Understanding Globalization* (Second Edition), Lanham: Rowman & Littlefield

Schuurman 2001 Schuurman, F. ed. *Globalization and Development Studies* London: Sage

Seabrook 1996 Seabrook, J. *In the Cities of the South* London: Verso

Sen 1999 Sen, A. *Development as Freedom* Oxford: Oxford University Press

Shanks 2008 Shanks, A. *Against Innocence* London: SCM

Sine 1999 Sine, T. *Mustard Seed versus McWorld* London:Monarch

Singer 2003 Singer, P. *Pushing Time Away* London: Granta

Smith A. 1995 Smith, A.D. *Nations and Nationalism in a Global Era*, Cambridge: Polity Press

Smith D. 2003 Smith, D. *Mission After Christendom*, London: Dartman, Longman & Todd

Sontag 2009 Sontag, S. *Under the Sign of Saturn* London: Penguin

Stackhouse 2000 Stackhouse J., *Out of Poverty and Into Something More Comfortable*, Random House Canada

Stiglitz 2002 Stiglitz, J. *Globalization and its Discontents* London: Penguin

Surgirtharajah 2003 Surgirtharajah, R.S. *Post-colonial Reconfigurations* London: SCM

Thomas 2008 Thomas, M. *Belching Out the Devil* London: Ebury Press

Toynbee 2003 Toynbee, P. *Hard Work* London: Bloomsbury

Vargas Llosa 1991 Vargas Llosa, M. *The Storyteller* London: Faber

Weatherhead 1934 Weatherhead, L. *Psychology and Life* , London: Hodder & Stoughton, 1934

Wehling 2002 Wehling, P. 'Dynamic Constellations of the Individual, Society and Nature, Critical Theory and Environmental Sociology' in Dunlap, Buttel, Dickens & Gijswijt eds. *Sociological Theory and the Environment*, Oxford: Rowman and Littlefield

Weil 2001 Weil, S. *Oppression and Liberty* London: Routledge

Weil 2002 Weil, S. *The Need for Roots* London: Routledge

Werbner 2002 Werbner R. (ed.) *Postcolonial Subjectivities in Africa*, London: Zed Books

Wilkinson & Pickett 2010 Wilkinson R. and Pickett, K. *The Spirit Level: Why More Equal Societies Almost Always Do Better* London: Penguin

Williams 1988a   Williams, R., *Border Country*, London: Hogarth Press

Williams 1988b   Williams, R., *Second Generation*, London: Hogarth Press

Williams 1988c   Williams, R. *The Fight for Manod*, London: Hogarth Press

Williams 1989   Williams, R., *Loyalties* London: Hogarth Press

Williams 1990   Williams R. *People of the Black Mountains 1 The Beginning* London; Paladin

Williams 1992   Williams R. *People of the Black Mountains 2 The Eggs of the Eagle* London; Paladin

Wink 1992   Wink, W. *Engaging the Powers* Minneapolis: Fortress Press

Wright 1996   Wright, N.T. *Jesus and the Victory of God* London: SPCK

INDEX